SINGER

SEWING REFERENCE LIBRARY®

Quick & Easy Decorating Projects

Cy DeCosse Incorporated
Minnetonka, Minnesota

Quick & Easy
Decorating
Projects

Contents

CY DECOSSE INCORPORATED

A COWLES MAGAZINES COMPANY

Chairman/CEO: Bruce Barnet
Chairman Emeritus: Cy DeCosse
President/COO: Nino Tarantino
Executive V. P./Editor-in-Chief:
  William B. Jones

Copyright © 1995
Cy DeCosse Incorporated
5900 Green Oak Drive
Minnetonka, Minnesota 55343
1-800-328-3895
All rights reserved
Printed in U.S.A.

QUICK & EASY DECORATING
PROJECTS
Created by: The Editors of Cy DeCosse
Incorporated, in cooperation with
the Sewing Education Department,
Singer Sewing Company. Singer is a
trademark of The Singer Company
and is used under license.

Library of Congress
Cataloging-in-Publication Data

Quick & easy decorating projects.

p. cm. — (Singer sewing reference library)
Includes index.
ISBN 0-86573-302-3
ISBN 0-86573-303-1 (softcover)
1. Household linens. 2. Machine
sewing. 3. Interior decoration.
I. Title: Quick and easy decorating
projects
TT387.Q85 1995
646.2'1 — dc20   94-49671

Also available from the publisher:
*Sewing Essentials, Sewing for the Home,
Clothing Care & Repair, Sewing for Style,
Sewing Specialty Fabrics, Sewing
Activewear, The Perfect Fit, Timesaving
Sewing, More Sewing for the Home,
Tailoring, Sewing for Children, Sewing
with an Overlock, 101 Sewing Secrets,
Sewing Pants That Fit, Quilting by
Machine, Decorative Machine Stitching,
Creative Sewing Ideas, Sewing Lingerie,
Sewing Projects for the Home, Sewing with
Knits, More Creative Sewing Ideas, Quilt
Projects by Machine, Creating Fashion
Accessories, Quick & Easy Sewing Projects,
Sewing for Special Occasions, Sewing for
the Holidays*

Group Executive Editor: Zoe A. Graul
Senior Technical Director: Rita C. Arndt
Technical Director: Dawn M. Anderson
Project Manager: Tracy Stanley
Assistant Project Manager: Amy Berndt
Senior Art Director: Delores Swanson
Art Director: Linda Schloegel
Writer: Dawn M. Anderson
Editor: Janice Cauley
Sample Production Manager: Carol Olson
Photo Coordinator: Elaine Johnson
Styling Director: Bobbette Destiche
Senior Technical Photo Stylist: Bridget
 Haugh
Technical Photo Stylists: Phyllis Galbraith,
 Susan Jorgensen, Nancy Sundeen
Project Stylist: Joanne Wawra
Research Assistants: Linda Neubauer,
 Lori Ritter
Sewing Staff: Sharon Eklund, Corliss
 Forstrom, Phyllis Galbraith, Valerie
 Hill, Kristi Kuhnau, Virginia Mateen,

Linda Neubauer, Carol Pilot, Nancy
 Sundeen, Michelle Skudlarek
*V. P. Development Planning
 & Production:* Jim Bindas
Production Manager: Laurie Gilbert
Director of Photography: Mike Parker
Creative Photo Coordinator: Cathleen
 Shannon
Studio Manager: Marcia Chambers
Lead Photographer: Chuck Nields
Photographers: Stuart Block, Rebecca
 Hawthorne, Kevin Hedden, Mike
 Hehner, Rex Irmen, Billy Lindner,
 Mark Macemon, Paul Najlis, Mike
 Parker, Robert Powers, Greg Wallace
Contributing Photographers: Phil
 Aarestad, Paul Englund, Brian
 Holman, Mette Nielsen, Steve Smith
Desktop Publishing Specialist: Laurie
 Kristensen
Production Staff: Deborah Eagle,
 Kevin Hedden, Mike Hehner, Rob

Johnstone, Phil Juntti, Jeannette Moss,
 John Nadeau, Mike Peterson, Mike
 Schauer, Greg Wallace, Kay Wethern,
 Nik Wogstad
Consultants: Lana Bennett, Joyce Eide,
 Amy Engman, Wendy Fedie, Pamela
 Hastings, Susan Stein
Contributors: Coats & Clark Inc.; Concord
 House, Division of Concord Fabrics
 Inc.; EZ International; HTC-Handler
 Textile Corporation; Kirsch; Olfa®
 Products International; Spartex Inc.;
 Swiss-Metrosene, Inc.; V.I.P Fabrics,
 Division of Cranston Print Works
 Company; Waverly, Division of
 Schumacher & Company
Printed on American paper by:
R. R. Donnelley & Sons Co. (0595)

Introduction

Swagged triangle valances (page 19).

Quick & Easy Decorating Projects is filled with ideas to brighten your home. Included are simple window treatments, projects for bedrooms and bathrooms, ideas for furniture cover-ups, and decorative accessories to use in any room.

The Window Treatments section contains many top treatments, such as a valance with clustered gathers, a swagged triangle valance, or a valance with an attached flounce. These valances can be used alone, or over shades or blinds. For a romantic look, make a valance with a swag and two cascades from a purchased lace tablecloth. For privacy, sew simple buttonhole curtain panels that slide onto a rod through buttonholes.

In the Bed & Bath section, you will find a flanged duvet cover, a banded bed skirt, and a decorative sheet flap with matching pillowcases. Make pillow shams with bordered insets for standard bed pillows or pillow shams with buttoned flaps, designed to fit European square

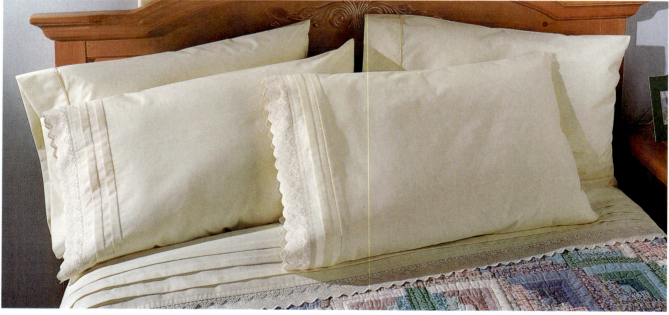

Decorative sheet flap and pillowcases (page 54).

bed pillows. For a new look in the bathroom, make an easy shower curtain from a decorative sheet, and a terry bath mat.

The Cover-ups section features simple coverings for furniture and accessories, such as a reversible chair seat cover, lamp shade covers, and a ruffled table cover for a side table or sofa table. For the dining table, sew a tablecloth and placemats with lace edging, or a two-way table runner.

The Finishing Touches section includes easy room accessories. Bordered pillows, pillows with knotted ties, and sphere pillows make attractive decorating accents. Or try a no-sew fringed pillow made from casement fabric. For fun, make a beanbag chair for a child or an adult. There is also a synthetic fur throw and a simple pieced lap quilt.

Use the symbols below to estimate the time needed to complete the projects in this book.

= an evening (2 to 4 hours)

= a day (4 to 6 hours)

= a weekend (8 or more hours)

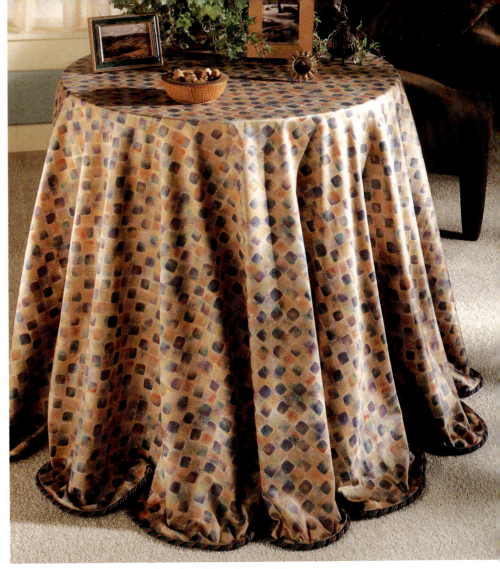

Round tablecloth with twisted welting (page 85).

Envelope pillows (page 104).

Window Treatments

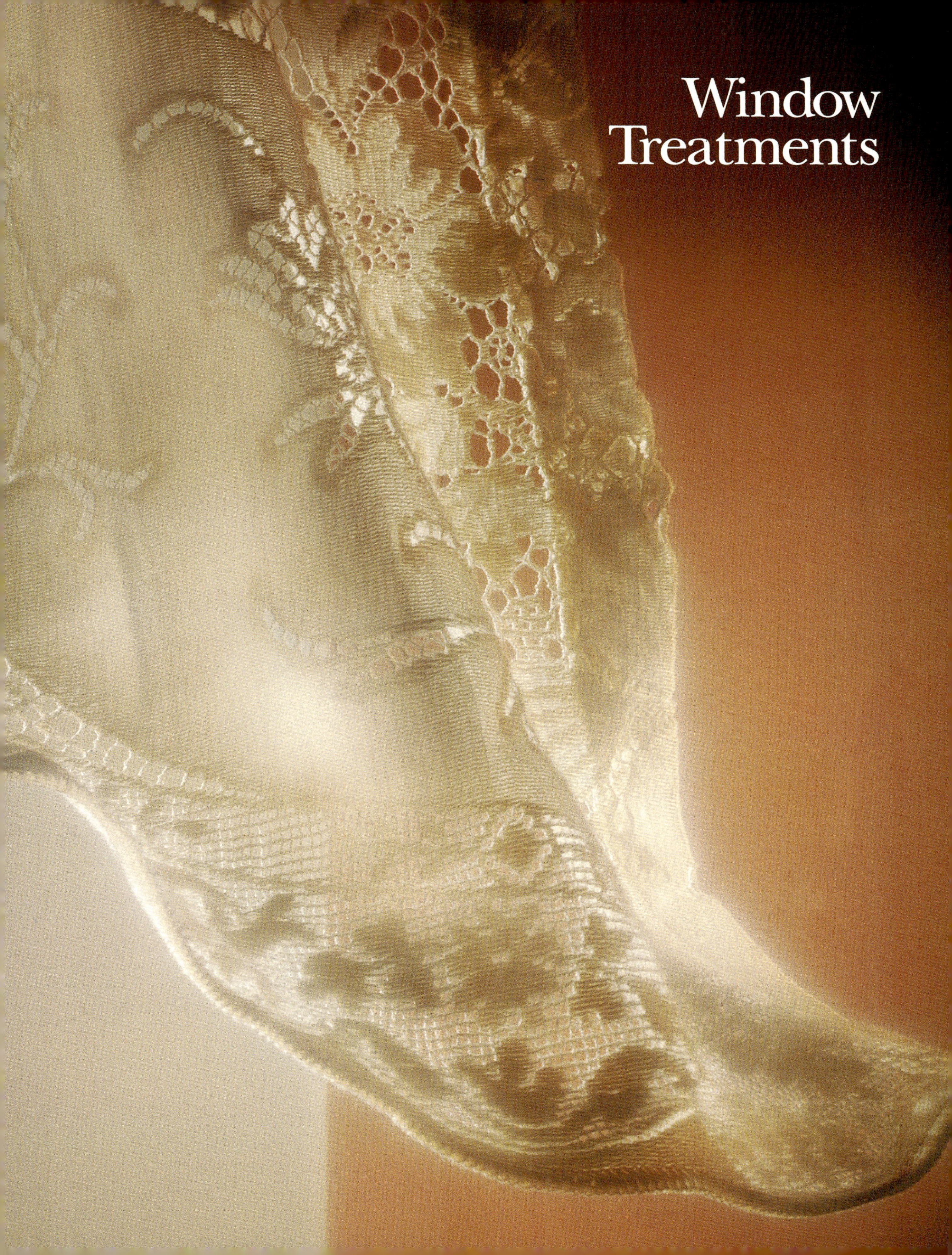

Valances with Clustered Gathers

Valances with clustered gathers are simple top treatments that may be used with shades or blinds. Soft, clustered gathers are spaced evenly across the width of the valance, and decorative cording, knotted at each cluster, is used for embellishment.

The valance is mounted outside the window frame on a mounting board that can be positioned at the top of the window frame or on the wall above the window. The finished width of the valance should be at least 2" (5 cm) wider than the outside measurement of the window frame. If there is no undertreatment, a 1 × 3 board can be used. With an undertreatment, use a mounting board that will project out from the window frame enough so the valance will clear the undertreatment by 1" to 2" (2.5 to 5 cm).

For attractive gathers, make the valance from a soft decorator fabric. For nondirectional prints, the valance may be constructed on the crosswise grain. For directional prints, piece the fabric as necessary, matching the pattern. Plan the placement of seams to fall within a cluster of gathers, if possible. The valance is constructed with a self-lining; therefore, a pattern printed on lightweight or light-colored fabric may show through to the right side. Test the fabric by folding a piece in half and holding it up to a light or a window to see if the pattern shows through.

✂ Cutting Directions

The cut width of the fabric is equal to the length of the mounting board plus two times the width, or projection, of the mounting board plus 1" (2.5 cm) for ½" (1.3 cm) seam allowances plus 6" (15 cm) for each clustered gather. Space clustered gathers from 7" to 10" (18 to 25.5 cm) apart along the front of the mounting board.

The cut length of the fabric is equal to two times the desired length of the valance plus 1" (2.5 cm) for ½" (1.3 cm) seam allowances; the finished length of the valance may range from 12" to 16" (30.5 to 40.5 cm), depending on the size of the window.

YOU WILL NEED

Decorator fabric.	**Angle irons,** one for each end of mounting board and one for every 45" (115 cm) interval across the width of the board.
Cording.	
Mounting board.	
Heavy-duty stapler.	**Pan-head screws** or molly bolts.

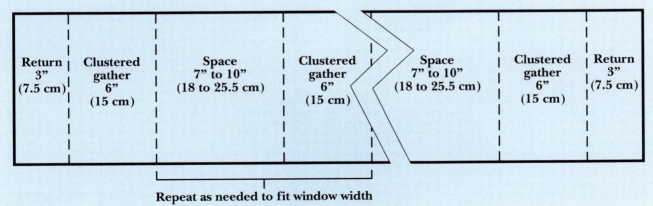

Return 3" (7.5 cm)	Clustered gather 6" (15 cm)	Space 7" to 10" (18 to 25.5 cm)	Clustered gather 6" (15 cm)	Space 7" to 10" (18 to 25.5 cm)	Clustered gather 6" (15 cm)	Return 3" (7.5 cm)

Repeat as needed to fit window width

Determine the number and spacing of clustered gathers and the amount of fabric needed for the *returns* that wrap around the sides of the mounting board, using the guide above. Plan for a clustered gather at each end of the board; space additional clustered gathers about 7" to 10" (18 to 25.5 cm) apart. Allow 6" (15 cm) of fabric for each clustered gather.

How to Sew a Valance with Clustered Gathers

1) Seam fabric widths, if necessary. Fold the fabric in half lengthwise, with right sides together and raw edges even; pin. Stitch ½" (1.3 cm) from raw edges; leave 8" (20.5 cm) opening on upper edge for turning.

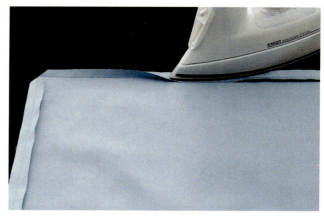

2) Trim corners diagonally. Press the seam allowances open at edges. Turn the valance right side out. Press edges, folding in the seam allowances at the opening. Slipstitch opening closed.

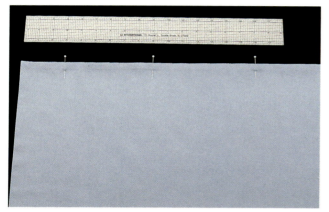

3) Pin-mark a distance equal to width of mounting board on each end of valance at seamed upper edge. Pin-mark placement of clustered gathers at the upper edge of the valance.

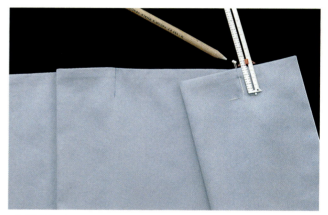

4) Fold pleat in valance, matching pin marks for each clustered gather. Mark a line parallel to fold, 1½" (3.8 cm) deep at pin mark. Stitch in place on the marked line. Repeat for remaining clustered gathers.

5) Check fit of valance around the mounting board. Adjust pleats, if necessary for accurate fit.

6) Hand-gather fabric in pleat area 1" (2.5 cm) from upper edge; secure with hand stitching. Repeat for remaining clustered gathers.

7) Mark center of mounting board around edges on sides and face of board, using pencil. Mark valance 1" (2.5 cm) from upper edge, using chalk pencil.

8) Staple valance to board, aligning marked line on board with marked line on valance; place staples between clustered gathers.

9) Unravel the ends of cording so individual cords lie parallel and flat; secure the ends with masking tape. Staple taped ends to back side of mounting board.

10) Tie a knot in cording to align with first cluster; secure cording to valance over the staples, using hot glue. Hold cording in place on both sides of cluster until glue sets.

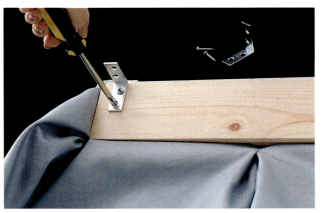

11) Continue knotting and securing remainder of cording to the valance. Secure ends of cording and staple to back of board as in step 9.

12) Secure angle irons to the bottom of mounting board, near ends and at 45" (115 cm) intervals, using pan-head screws. Secure angle irons to top of window frame or into the wall studs, using pan-head screws; if securing to drywall or plaster, use molly bolts.

Overlapping Triangle Valances ✺

An overlapping triangle valance is a simple lined treatment made from two panels attached to a mounting board. Welting accents the diagonal edge of the panels.

Mount the valance on a 1 × 3 board no longer than 50½" (128.3 cm) or a 1 × 4 board no longer than 49½" (126.3 cm). The standard-size boards actually measure about ¾" × 2½" (2 × 6.5 cm) and ¾" × 3½" (2 × 9 cm), respectively. The lengths given are the maximum for which the panels can be constructed using a single width of 54" (137 cm) fabric.

The mounting board can be mounted either at the top of the window frame or on the wall above the window. The finished width of the valance should be at least 2" (5 cm) wider than the outside measurement of the window frame or 2" (5 cm) wider than the width of an undertreatment. The finished length at the side of the valance and the depth, or projection, of the mounting board determine the angle of the panels and the depth of the overlap at the center.

Tape a length of string at the upper corners of the window and experiment with different side lengths to help determine the desired finished length.

✂ Cutting Directions

Cut two rectangles each from outer fabric and lining. The cut width of the rectangles is equal to the length of the mounting board plus the depth, or projection, of the mounting board for one return plus 1" (2.5 cm) for seam allowances. The cut length of the rectangles is equal to the finished length of the valance plus the depth of the mounting board plus ½" (1.3 cm) for seam allowance. The rectangles are cut to size on page 16, steps 1 to 3.

YOU WILL NEED

Decorator fabric; two coordinating fabrics may be used.

Lining fabric.

Purchased welting.

Mounting board.

Heavy-duty stapler; staples.

Angle irons; pan-head screws or molly bolts.

How to Sew an Overlapping Triangle Valance

1) **Place** one piece each of fabric and lining wrong sides together. On right side of fabric, ½" (1.3 cm) from side edge, measure from upper edge, the width of the mounting board plus ½" (1.3 cm); mark point.

2) **Draw** line from lower left corner through point at upper right to mark lower edge of left valance panel and lining. Cut on marked line; discard excess fabric.

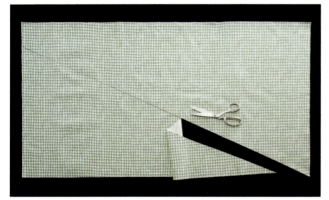

3) **Repeat** steps 1 and 2 to cut the right valance panel and lining; mark and cut diagonal lower edge at angle opposite that of left panel. Set aside lining panels until step 7.

4) **Pin** welting to right side of the outer fabric along diagonal lower edge; position stitching line of welting ½" (1.3 cm) from raw edge of fabric. Trim ends of welting even with edges of fabric.

5) **Pull** the cording at each end and trim away about ⅝" (1.5 cm), to reduce bulk in the seam allowance. Smooth welting in place.

6) **Baste** welting to valance, using a zipper foot and ½" (1.3 cm) seam allowance.

7) **Pin** lining to the outer fabric, with right sides together and raw edges even. With outer fabric up, stitch around sides and lower edges in ½" (1.3 cm) seam; at diagonal edge, stitch just inside previous stitching.

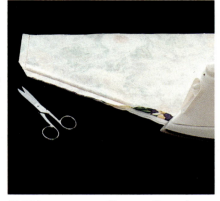

8) Trim corners diagonally; trim seam allowances at lower point. Press seam allowances open.

9) Turn valance right side out; press. Smooth layers flat; pin upper edges together. Finish upper edge, using overlock or zigzag stitch.

10) Measure from the side edge of panel the width of mounting board; fold to lining side. Lightly press to crease return. Repeat for remaining panel.

11) Align upper edge of right panel to back edge of the board, and position fold of return at right edge of the board; staple to within 6" (15 cm) of right edge of the board.

12) Make diagonal fold at the corner to fold in excess fullness; staple.

13) Repeat steps 11 and 12 to staple the left panel to the mounting board.

14) Secure angle irons to the bottom of mounting board, near ends, using pan-head screws. Secure angle irons to top of window frame or into wall studs, using pan-head screws; if securing to drywall or plaster, use molly bolts.

Swagged Triangle Valances

These stylish, swagged valances are simply squares of fabric folded in half and stitched to make self-lined triangles. The bias foldline at the upper edge creates a soft look. Corner grommets secure the valance panels to decorative hooks mounted in the top of the window frame. If desired, a small embellishment, such as a charm, bead, or tassel, can be hung from the lower point of each panel.

A single panel can be hung alone, or multiple panels can be overlapped for a layered effect. The finished size of the panel varies, depending on the space between the hooks and the amount of swag desired. The length of the panel from the folded edge to the lower point is about one-half the width of the panel at the upper edge. Determine the spacing, size, and number of panels desired by experimenting with triangles cut from test fabric. For a large window, use the design of the window as a guide for determining the number of panels to use.

✂ Cutting Directions

Determine the size of the triangle panels, and cut the panels as on page 20, steps 1 to 3.

YOU WILL NEED

Decorator fabric.

Test fabric, such as muslin; tape.

Grommets, size 1; grommet attaching tool.

Embellishment, such as a charm, bead, or tassel, for each valance panel, optional.

Decorative cording or ribbon, for securing embellishment.

Swagged triangle valances create a simple draped look at the top of the window. Above, several overlapping panels are used to cover a large window. Each panel is embellished with beads at the lower point. Opposite, a single panel is embellished with a cherry cluster.

How to Sew a Swagged Triangle Valance

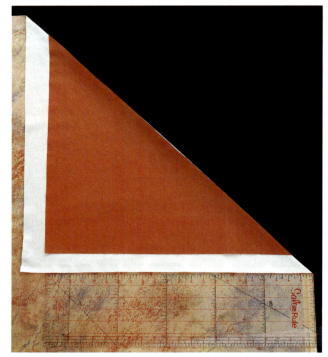

1) Cut right triangles from test fabric with diagonal line on the bias. Tape triangles to window frame, and experiment with placement until desired look is achieved. Recut right triangle from test fabric to size.

2) Fold fabric on the bias, right sides together. Position the test fabric triangle on fabric with diagonal side of triangle on fold of fabric.

3) Place a straightedge at a 45° angle to the fold; mark cutting line for side of panel, ½" (1.3 cm) from edge of test fabric as shown. Repeat for the opposite side. Cut on marked lines.

4) Pin sides of triangle panel, right sides together, along raw edges. Stitch ½" (1.3 cm) from raw edges, leaving a 5" to 6" (12.5 to 15 cm) opening along one side; at lower point (inset), take one or two short stitches diagonally across corner.

5) Taper the seam allowances at the points. Press the seams open.

6) Turn valance right side out; push points out gently with a point turner. Slipstitch opening closed. Press sides of panel; do not press upper edge.

7) Attach a grommet at each upper corner of the triangle panel, about 1" (2.5 cm) from the lower and upper edges.

8) Attach grommet at the lower point, if desired; tie embellishment to grommet, using decorative cording or ribbon.

Valances with Attached Flounces 🌙

This valance, which has two layers of softly gathered fabric, is quick and easy to sew. Two strips of fabric are stitched into a long tube. A contrasting band is cleverly created by simply folding the fabric tube; then a rod pocket is stitched along the length of the tube. When the fabric is gathered onto the rod, the upper portion of the valance falls gracefully over the rod, creating a flounce with a banded edge.

Two different looks can be achieved. For a tailored style (above), a crisp fold is pressed at the lower edge of the valance. For a pouf style (opposite), the valance is cut a little longer, and the fabric layers are separated for a soft look. Both valances have a finished length of about 11" (28 cm).

✂ Cutting Directions

For a tailored valance, you will need one strip each of the valance fabric and the flounce fabric. Determine the cut width of the fabric strips by multiplying the length of the rod by two and one-half; if it is necessary to piece the fabric widths together, also add 1" (2.5 cm) for each seam. The cut length of the valance fabric is 31" (78.5 cm); the cut length of the flounce fabric is 7" (18 cm).

For the pouf valance, you will need one strip each of the valance fabric and the flounce fabric. Determine the cut width of the fabric strips by multiplying the length of the rod by two and one-half; if it is necessary to piece the fabric widths together, also add 1" (2.5 cm) for each seam. The cut length of the valance fabric is 32" (81.5 cm); the cut length of the flounce fabric is 6" (15 cm).

YOU WILL NEED

Two coordinating decorator fabrics.
Curtain rod, 2½" (6.5 cm) wide.

Pouf valance is created by separating the fabric layers for a soft look. The tailored valance (top) is pressed flat along the lower edge for a crisp finish.

How to Sew a Valance with an Attached Flounce

Tailored Valance. 1) Seam valance fabric widths, if necessary, using ½" (1.3 cm) seam allowances and matching any pattern as on page 39; repeat for flounce. Press seams open.

2) Pin lower edge of flounce strip to the upper edge of valance strip, right sides together. Stitch ½" (1.3 cm) seam; press seam allowance toward the flounce.

3) Pin the remaining long edge of the flounce strip to the valance strip, right sides together, forming a tube. Stitch ½" (1.3 cm) seam; press seam allowance toward valance fabric.

4) Press under 1" (2.5 cm) twice on both ends of tube; stitch around tube, close to fold, to make double-fold side hems.

5) Turn tube right side out; press a fold ½" (1.3 cm) from seamline at lower edge of flounce, forming a contrasting band; edge of seam allowance is at foldline. Stitch in the ditch along band by stitching over the seamline in the well of the seam.

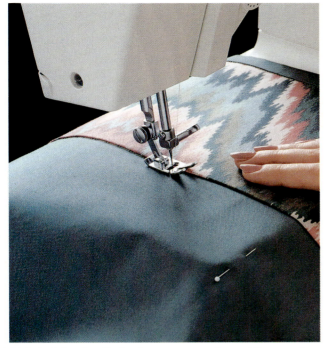

6) Stitch in the ditch along upper edge of flounce by stitching over the seamline in the well of the seam.

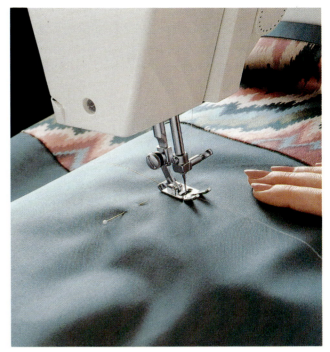

7) Mark a chalk line 3" (7.5 cm) from upper edge of flounce. Stitch on marked line, through both layers of valance fabric, forming a rod pocket.

8) Press a fold at lower edge of valance. Insert rod through rod pocket, gathering fabric evenly; fold the flounce to outside. Hang valance; adjust flounce.

Pouf valance. Follow steps 1 to 7, opposite. Insert rod through rod pocket, gathering the fabric evenly; fold flounce to outside. Hang valance; adjust flounce. Pull valance fabric layers apart along length of valance, to create poufs.

Valances from Lace Tablecloths ☀

Create shirred valances using oval lace tablecloths with decorative, shaped edges. One oval tablecloth is cut to make the swag and two cascade panels for this valance, as shown on page 28. The only sewing required is stitching the rod pocket and the side hems on the cascades.

This valance is best suited for wide windows. The length and width of the swag and cascades varies with the size of the tablecloth and the depth of the rod pocket and heading.

To determine the tablecloth size to use, allow for one and three-fourths to two and one-half times fullness. Add the width and length of the tablecloth; then subtract 4" (10 cm) for the side hems of the cascades. Divide this measurement by 1.75 to 2.5, to determine the range of window widths for this tablecloth size. The chart on the opposite page lists common oval tablecloth sizes and the window widths they will cover.

The cut length of the swag panel is equal to one-half the width, or shortest dimension, of the tablecloth, because the tablecloth is cut in half lengthwise. The cut length of the cascade panels is equal to one-half the length, or longest dimension, of the tablecloth. The finished length of the valance panels, from the top of the heading to the lower edge, is equal to the

cut length of the panels minus a 1" to 2" (2.5 to 5 cm) heading depth minus the rod pocket depth minus ½" (1.3 cm) turn-under. The rod pocket depth is one-half the measurement around the rod plus ¼" (6 mm) for ease. If desired, the swag panel can be cut shorter; usually this also decreases the width of the panel.

✂ Cutting Directions

Determine the necessary tablecloth size; then cut the panels as on page 28, steps 1 and 2.

YOU WILL NEED

Oval lace tablecloth.
Decorative curtain rod or pole set.

Tablecloth and Window Measurements

Common oval tablecloth sizes	Window widths
52" × 70" (132 × 178 cm)	47" to 67" (120 to 170.5 cm)
60" × 84" (152.5 × 213.5 cm)	56" to 80" (142 to 203.5 cm)
60" × 92" (152.5 × 234 cm)	59" to 85" (149.8 to 216 cm)
60" × 104" (152.5 × 264.5 cm)	64" to 91" (163 to 231.5 cm)
70" × 108" (178 × 274.5 cm)	70" to 99" (178 to 251.5 cm)
70" × 126" (178 × 320 cm)	78" to 110" (198 to 280 cm)

Cutting Plan for a Valance from an Oval Lace Tablecloth

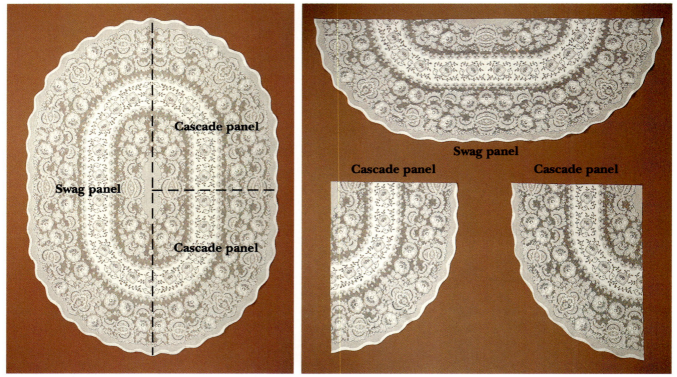

Oval tablecloth is cut to make the swag and two cascade panels for this valance, as shown. The tablecloth is cut in steps 1 and 2, below.

How to Sew a Valance from an Oval Lace Tablecloth

1) Fold the lace tablecloth in half lengthwise; cut along the fold.

2) Set aside one tablecloth section for the swag panel. Fold remaining section in half crosswise; cut along fold to make two cascade panels.

3) Adjust the length of swag, if desired, by trimming desired amount from upper cut edges. Turn up 1" (2.5 cm) twice to wrong side on side edge of cascade; stitch close to the inner fold. Repeat on remaining cascade, making sure panel is reverse of first panel.

4) Press up ½" (1.3 cm) to wrong side on upper edge. Then press up an amount equal to rod-pocket depth plus heading depth; take up fullness with small tucks on each side or ease in any excess fullness.

5) Stitch close to inner fold. Stitch again at depth of heading, using seam guide or tape on bed of sewing machine as guide for stitching.

6) Repeat steps 4 and 5 on the cut edge of the swag panel.

7) Insert pole or curtain rod into rod pockets, gathering the fabric evenly. Hang valance.

Buttonhole Curtain Panels

Simple in style, these no-fuss, unlined curtains have fresh appeal. The flat fabric panels slide onto the curtain rod through buttonholes, creating a curtain with soft, rolling curves.

✂ Cutting Directions

Determine the desired finished length of the panels by measuring from ½" (1.3 cm) above the top of the rod to the desired finished length of the curtain. Determine the necessary length of the buttonholes; the buttonhole length is equal to one-half the measurement around the rod plus ¼" (6 mm).

The facing and turn-under at the top of the panel is equal to the length of the buttonholes plus 1½" (3.8 cm). The hem allowance at the bottom is equal to 6" (15 cm); this allows for a 3" (7.5 cm) double-fold hem. The cut length of each panel is equal to the desired finished length plus the facing and turn-under at the top plus the hem allowance at the bottom.

Determine the cut width of the fabric by multiplying the length of the rod times two; if you are sewing two curtain panels, divide this measurement by two to determine the cut width of each panel. For each panel, add 4" (10 cm) to allow for 1" (2.5 cm) double-fold side hems; if it is necessary to piece the fabric widths together, also add 1" (2.5 cm) for each seam.

YOU WILL NEED

Lightweight to mediumweight decorator fabric.
Pole set or decorative curtain rod.

How to Sew a Buttonhole Curtain Panel

1) Seam fabric widths, if necessary, for each curtain panel. Trim seam allowances to ¼" (6 mm); finish, using zigzag or overlock stitch, and press to one side. At lower edge, press under 3" (7.5 cm) twice to wrong side; stitch close to inner fold.

2) Press under ½" (1.3 cm) on the upper edge. Then press under an amount equal to buttonhole length plus 1" (2.5 cm). Stitch close to inner fold.

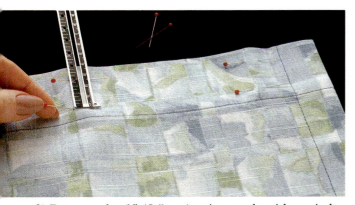

3) Press under 1" (2.5 cm) twice on the sides; stitch close to the inner fold. Pin-mark placement for even number of buttonholes on top of panel, centered on faced area; space end buttonholes 2" (5 cm) from sides, and remaining buttonholes 4" to 5" (10 to 12.5 cm) apart.

4) Stitch vertical buttonholes. Weave panels onto pole or rod. Hang curtains.

Bed & Bath

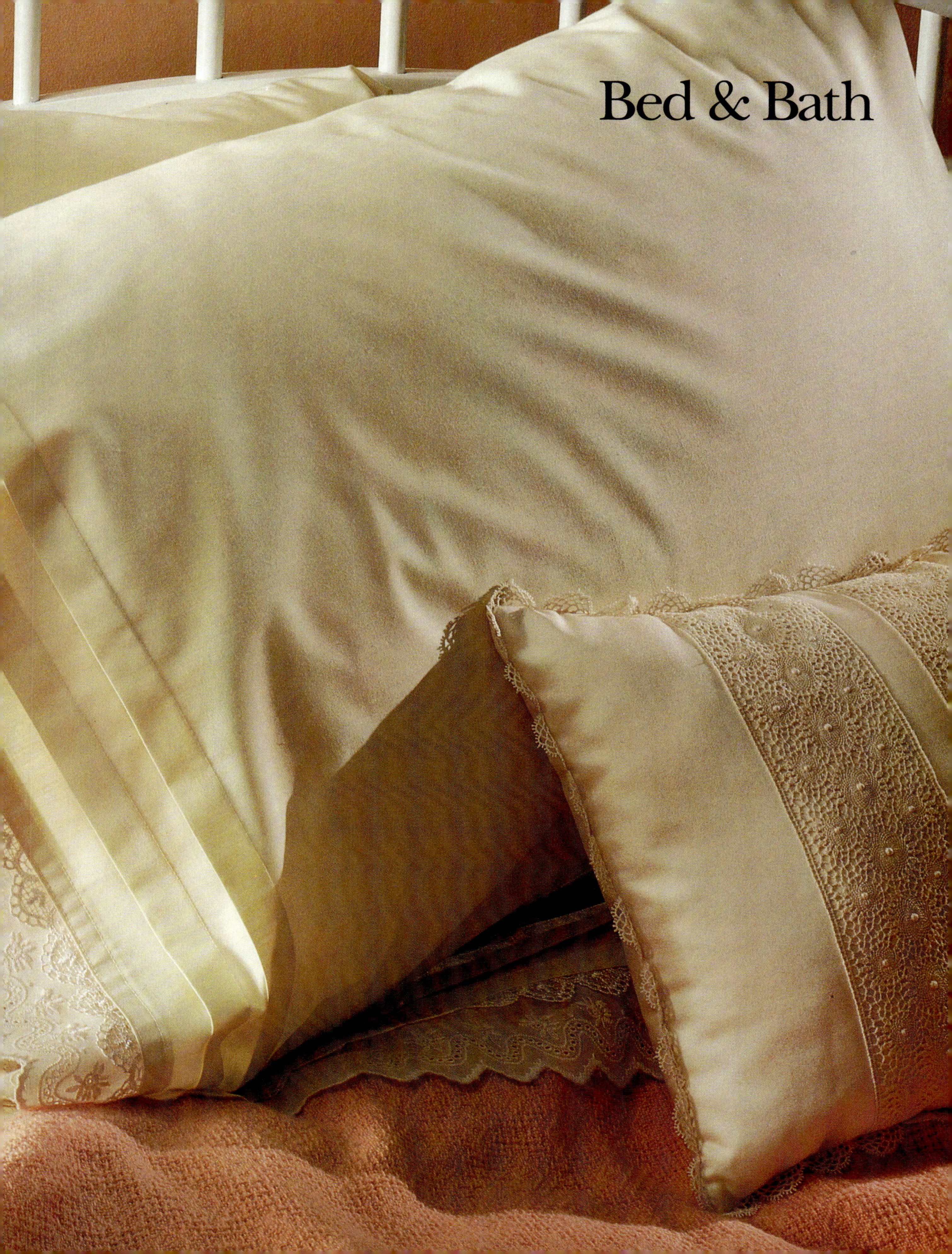

Lined Bedspreads & Coverlets ✺✺

Basic bedspreads and coverlets with bound lower edges are easily made from decorator fabrics. The lining and binding can be made from contrasting decorator fabrics for a coordinated look. The lining gives the bedspread or coverlet extra body, and the wide binding provides a decorative touch. For easier sewing, choose a mediumweight, tightly woven cotton or cotton-blend fabric, such as sateen or chintz.

Two or more widths of fabric are needed, depending on the size of the bed and the fabric width. Decorator fabrics are usually 48" or 54" (122 or 137 cm) wide. Always center one full width of fabric on the top of the bed, and seam equal partial widths on each side.

To determine the finished length and width of the bedspread or coverlet, measure the bed over the blankets and sheets that will normally be used. As shown below, measure the length of the bed from the head to the foot (a). Allow an extra 15" to 20" (38 to 51 cm) in length if the bedspread or coverlet will tuck under and wrap over the pillows. Measure the width of the bed from side to side (b). For a bedspread, measure the drop length (c), from the top of the mattress to the floor; then subtract ½" (1.3 cm) for clearance. For a coverlet, measure the drop length (d), from the top of the mattress to the desired finished length, 1" to 4" (2.5 to 10 cm) below the top of the box spring.

To determine the amount of fabric needed, first calculate the number of widths needed by dividing the cut width of the bedspread or coverlet by the fabric width; round off to the next highest number. Multiply the number of widths by the cut length to determine the amount of fabric needed. Additional fabric may be necessary for matching patterns.

✀ Cutting Directions

The cut length of the bedspread or coverlet is equal to the finished length from the head of the bed to the foot, including any additional length for tucking under and wrapping over the pillow, plus the drop length. Add ½" (1.3 cm) for the seam at the upper edge.

The cut width of the bedspread or coverlet after the panels are pieced together is equal to the width of the bed plus twice the drop length. Cut bias strips of the binding fabric 4" (10 cm) wide; cut enough strips to equal twice the finished length of the bedspread or coverlet, plus the finished width plus 1½" (3.8 cm) for finishing ends.

YOU WILL NEED

Decorator fabric, for top of bedspread or coverlet.
Decorator fabric, for lining.
1½ yd. (1.4 m) decorator fabric, for binding.

How to Sew a Lined Bedspread or Coverlet

1) Seam widths of fabric together for the top of the bedspread, matching patterns, if necessary (page 39). Press seams open. Measure and cut bedspread top to exact finished width.

2) Repeat for the bedspread lining. Pin bedspread top to lining, right sides together, along upper edge. Stitch ½" (1.3 cm) seam; press open.

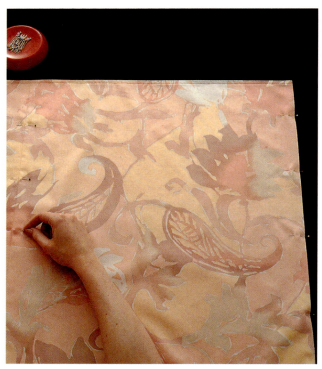

3) Turn bedspread right side out. Press along upper seam. Topstitch ¼" (6 mm) from seamed edge.

4) Pin bedspread top to lining, matching raw edges. Pin bedspread top to lining along seams, pinning at 4" to 6" (10 to 15 cm) intervals.

5) Topstitch ¼" (6 mm) from one side of one seam. Repeat on opposite side of seam, stitching from the same direction. Topstitch remaining seam.

6) Place the bedspread on the bed with equal drop length distributed on sides and foot of bed. Pin-mark one corner of bedspread along edge of mattress at foot of bed.

7) Fold bedspread in half lengthwise; place on a flat surface. Measure and mark the drop length out from pin marks in step 6, at 2" to 3" (5 to 7.5 cm) intervals, to mark the curve at the lower corners of bedspread.

8) Cut through two upper layers along marks. Cut two lower layers, using the upper layers as a guide; unfold. Repin bedspread top to lining around curves.

(Continued on next page)

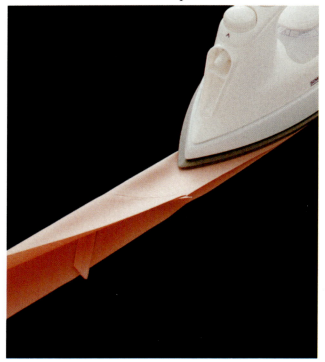

9) Sew bias binding strips together in ¼" (6 mm) seams; press open. Fold the binding strip in half lengthwise, wrong sides together; press along fold, taking care not to distort width of strip.

10) Pin binding strip to right side of the bedspread, matching raw edges; at the ends, allow ¾" (2 cm) to extend beyond upper edge. Ease in excess fullness so strip fits around curves.

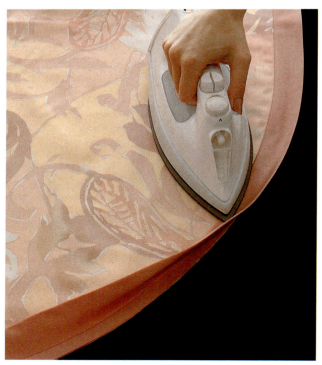

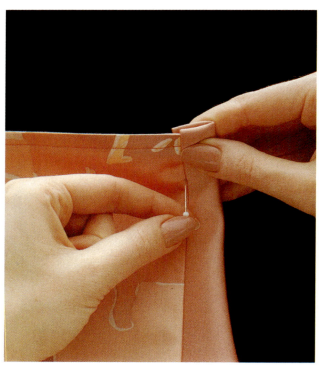

11) Stitch binding strip to bedspread ⅝" (1.5 cm) from edge. Press strip away from bedspread.

12) Fold end of binding strip over the upper edge of bedspread. Wrap binding around edge of bedspread, covering stitching line on back; pin.

13) Continue wrapping and pinning the binding around edge of the bedspread. Repeat step 12 for the remaining end.

14) Stitch in the ditch of the seam from the top of the bedspread, catching folded edge of binding strip on lining side. Hand-stitch across ends of binding at upper edge.

How to Match a Patterned Fabric

1) Position fabric widths, right sides together, matching selvages. Fold back the upper selvage until pattern matches; lightly press foldline.

2) Unfold selvage; pin fabric widths together on foldline. Check to see that the pattern matches from the right side.

3) Repin the fabric, so the pins are perpendicular to the foldline; stitch on the foldline, using straight stitch. Trim fabric to finished length.

Closure at the bottom of the duvet cover is created by overlapping the upper hemmed edges of the sheets and buttoning them in place.

Flanged Duvet Covers from Sheets ☀

Make an easy-to-sew flanged duvet cover from two flat sheets. The upper hemmed edge of the sheet used for the top of the cover wraps to the underside at the foot of the bed and buttons in place. Flanged duvet covers are constructed larger than the duvet; the duvet fills out the center portion and the flanged edges increase the size of the cover. Use this style with traditional down comforters, which are often too small to provide the drop length necessary to conceal the mattress at the sides and foot of the bed. The flange size may range from 2" to 5" (5 to 12.5 cm).

Refer to the cutting directions below and the diagram at right to determine the cut size of the sheets for the desired finished size of the duvet cover. Then refer to the sheet measurement chart (right) to determine the sheet sizes required. When making a cover for a twin-size or full-size bed, it may be necessary to purchase a queen-size sheet for the top of the cover in order to have enough length for the underlap and closure. The top of the cover must equal the desired finished length of the duvet cover plus 8" to 10" (20.5 to 25.5 cm) for the underlap and closure. Prewash the sheets before cutting.

✂ Cutting Directions

Measure the down duvet. For a flanged duvet cover, place the duvet on the bed and determine the desired finished size of the cover, including the drop length; the drop length at the sides of the bed is usually 9" to 12" (23 to 30.5 cm), depending on the mattress depth. Compare these measurements to the actual size of the duvet to determine the width of the flange on the sides and lower edge; the inside dimensions of the cover can be slightly smaller than the measurements of the duvet.

The cut width of the top and bottom sheets is equal to the desired finished width of the duvet cover plus 1" (2.5 cm) for two ½" (1.3 cm) seam allowances. The cut length of the top sheet is equal to the desired finished length of the duvet cover plus 8" to 10" (20.5 to 25.5 cm) for the underlap and closure and ½" (1.3 cm) for the seam allowance. The bottom sheet is cut to length on page 42, steps 2 and 3.

Cutting Diagram for Flanged Duvet Cover Top

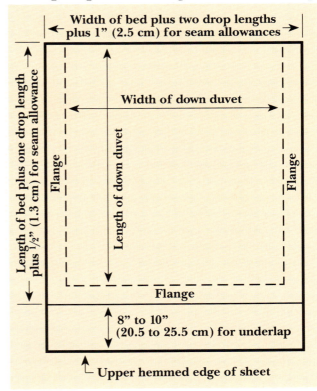

YOU WILL NEED

Two flat sheets.
Buttons.

Twill tape; four small plastic rings.

Standard Flat Sheets

Sheet Size	Measurements
Twin	66" × 96" (168 × 244 cm)
Full	81" × 96" (206 × 244 cm)
Queen	90" × 102" (229 × 259.5 cm)
King	108" × 102" (274.5 × 259.5 cm)

How to Sew a Flanged Duvet Cover from Sheets

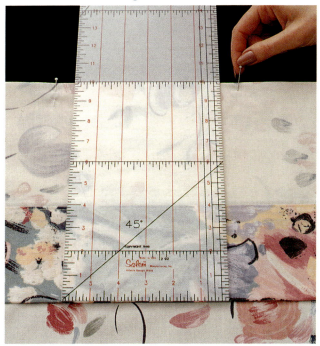

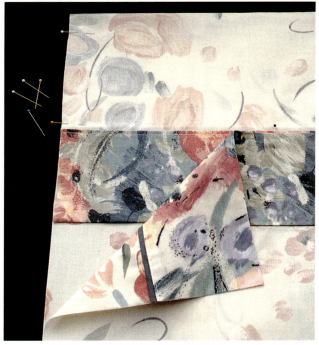

1) Place top sheet, right side up, on large, flat surface. On upper hemmed edge of sheet, fold 8" to 10" (20.5 to 25.5 cm) underlap, right sides together.

2) Place bottom sheet over the top sheet, right sides together, overlapping upper hemmed edges. Smooth sheets from the center out; pin layers together along sides and upper hemmed edge.

3) Turn sheets over; pin along lower edge. Trim lower edge of bottom sheet even with edge of top sheet. This edge will be at the upper edge of completed duvet cover.

4) Stitch ½" (1.3 cm) seam along the sides and the upper edge of duvet cover. Trim corners diagonally. Press seam allowances open.

5) Measure from edges of the duvet cover, and mark flange depth at each corner. Fold 20" (51 cm) strip of twill tape in half; baste to one layer of duvet cover at each marked corner as shown, so tape will be caught in stitching for flange.

6) Turn duvet cover right side out; press. Pin layers together. Measure from the edges of duvet cover, and mark depth of flange on sides and lower edge. Stitch on marked lines, pivoting at lower corners, to form flange; reinforce stitching at twill tape.

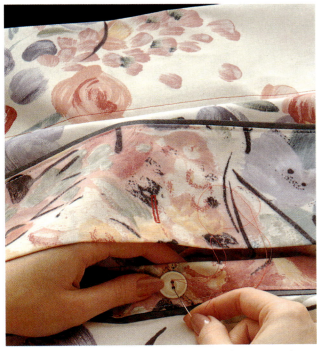

7) Mark the placement for the buttonholes on overlap, with end buttonholes about 6" (15 cm) from each side, and space remaining buttonholes about 12" (30.5 cm) apart. Stitch vertical buttonholes about ⅝" (1.5 cm) from folded edge. Stitch buttons to underlap.

8) Hand-stitch a plastic ring at each corner of duvet. Insert duvet in cover; secure twill tape to each ring with a bow.

Banded Bed Skirts 🌙

A contrasting band provides interest along the lower edges of a tailored bed skirt. For a romantic touch, add a lace overlay to the band. The side panels are designed to overlap the end panel at the corners to conceal the bed frame. The split at the corners allows the bed skirt to be used with beds that have footboards. For best results, construct the bed skirt from decorator fabrics that have body.

✂ Cutting Directions

For the upper bed skirt panels, cut one piece of fabric for each long side of the bed skirt, on the lengthwise grain, with the cut width of each piece equal to the length of the box spring plus 4" (10 cm), to allow for two 1" (2.5 cm) double-fold side hems. Cut one piece for the foot of the bed on the lengthwise grain, with the cut width equal to the width of the box spring plus

6" (15 cm), to allow for two 1" (2.5 cm) double-fold side hems and two 1" (2.5 cm) underlaps. The cut length of the upper bed skirt pieces is equal to the distance from the top of the box spring to the floor minus 2½" (6.5 cm).

For the contrasting band, cut three pieces, with the cut width equal to the cut width of the three upper bed skirt pieces. The cut length of the band pieces is 7" (18 cm); this allows for ½" (1.3 cm) clearance at the floor.

YOU WILL NEED

Decorator fabric, for upper bed skirt panels.
Contrasting decorator fabric, for band.
Fitted sheet.
Flat lace edging, for optional overlay.

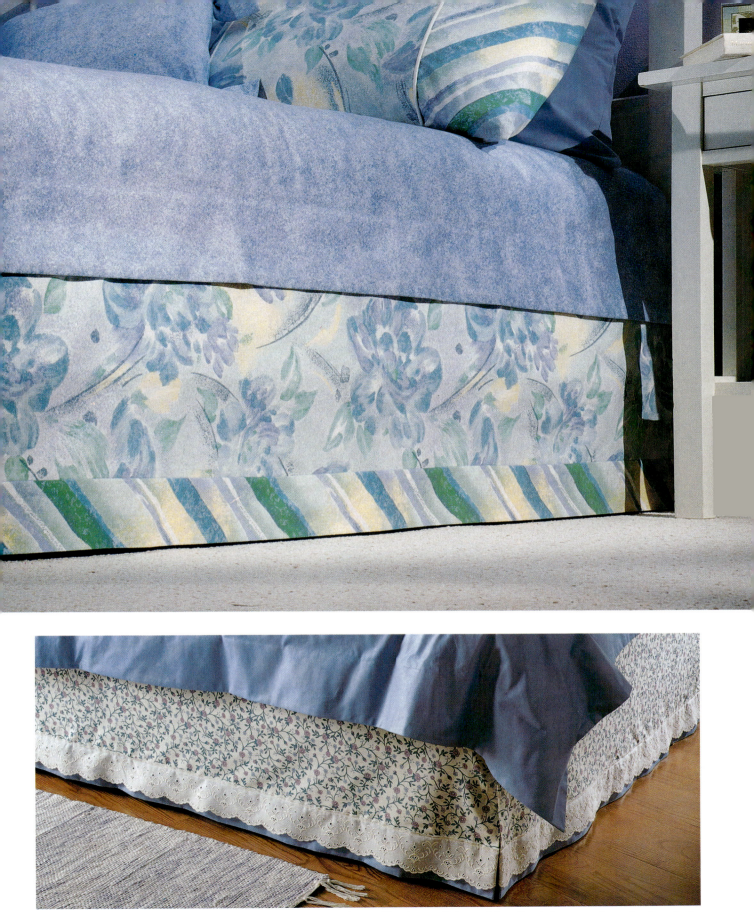

Banded bed skirts are made from two coordinating fabrics. Flat lace edging adds a feminine touch to the banded bed skirt above. Abstract prints are used for a contemporary look (top).

How to Sew a Banded Bed Skirt

1) **Place** fitted sheet over the box spring. Using water-soluble marking pen or chalk, mark sheet along upper edge of box spring on each side and on foot of bed. Mark the corners at center of curve.

2) **Press** the band pieces in half lengthwise, wrong sides together. Press ⅜" (1 cm) to the wrong side on one long edge of each band.

3) **Pin** band piece to lower edge of corresponding skirt piece, with right sides together and raw edges even. Stitch ½" (1.3 cm) seam. Press the seam allowance toward band.

4) **Fold** the band along center fold; the pressed edge extends about ⅛" (3 mm) beyond the stitching, concealing the seam allowance. Stitch in the ditch in the well of the seam on the right side, catching the band on the back side.

5) **Press** up 1" (2.5 cm) twice to wrong side on ends of panels; stitch close to inner folds. Finish upper edge, using zigzag or overlock stitch. Staystitch a scant ½" (1.3 cm) from upper edge of skirt pieces for 2" (5 cm) on each side.

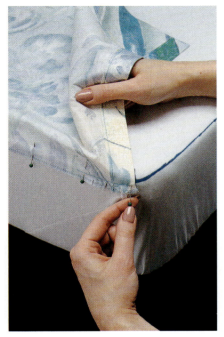

6) Lay the side pieces on top of the box spring, right side down; align ends with corner markings at foot of the bed. Pin upper edge of the bed skirt to the sheet, extending ½" (1.3 cm) seam allowance beyond marked line.

7) Lay panel for foot of bed on top of the box spring, right sides down, extending the ends 1" (2.5 cm) beyond the corner markings and overlapping side panels. Pin upper edge of bed skirt to sheet; clip the corners as necessary.

8) Remove the bed skirt and fitted sheet from bed. Stitch bed skirt to sheet, stitching ½" (1.3 cm) from raw edges.

How to Sew a Banded Bed Skirt with a Lace Overlay

1) Follow steps 1 to 5, opposite. Cut flat lace edging 2" (5 cm) longer than width of each skirt piece; finish ends, using zigzag or overlock stitch. Pin the lace to the skirt over band as desired, folding 1" (2.5 cm) at each end to back side. Topstitch in place.

2) Hand-stitch ends of lace in place. Stitch the lace to remaining skirt pieces. Complete the bed skirt as in steps 6 to 8.

Pillow Shams with Bordered Insets 🌙

The simple design of these pillow shams makes them suitable for many decorating styles. The pillow sham is easily constructed from three fabric panels that are pieced to create a bordered inset. Welting, stitched between the panels, provides additional detail. The side panels of the pillow sham fold to the back of the sham, creating an overlapping back closure. The pillow shams can be made to fit standard-size, queen-size, or king-size pillows.

✂ Cutting Directions

For each pillow sham, cut one center panel, one right side panel, and one left side panel, according to the chart, opposite.

YOU WILL NEED

Two coordinating decorator fabrics.
Purchased welting.

Cutting Chart for a Pillow Sham with a Bordered Inset

Pillow Size	Finished Size of Pillow Sham	Cut Size of Left Side Panel	Cut Size of Center Panel	Cut Size of Right Side Panel
Standard	20" × 26" (51 × 66 cm)	21" × 29" (53.5 × 73.5 cm)	21" × 15" (53.5 × 38 cm)	21" × 22" (53.5 × 56 cm)
Queen	20" × 30" (51 × 76 cm)	21" × 34" (53.5 × 86.5 cm)	21" × 17" (53.5 × 43 cm)	21" × 23" (53.5 × 58.5 cm)
King	20" × 36" (51 × 91.5 cm)	21" × 41" (53.5 × 104 cm)	21" × 21" (53.5 × 53.5 cm)	21" × 24" (53.5 × 61 cm)

How to Sew a Pillow Sham with a Bordered Inset

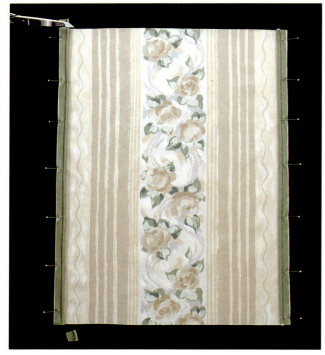

1) Pin welting to right side of center panel on side edges; position stitching line of welting ½" (1.3 cm) from raw edge of fabric. Trim the ends of welting even with edges of fabric.

2) Baste welting to center panel, using a zipper foot and ½" (1.3 cm) seam allowance.

3) Pin side panels to center panel, with right sides together and raw edges even. With the center panel facing up, stitch just inside previous stitching. Finish seams, using zigzag or overlock stitch. Press the seam allowances toward center panel.

4) Press ½" (1.3 cm), then 2" (5 cm), to the wrong side on short end of each side panel. Stitch close to inner fold.

5) Fold under fabric at sides to make side panels that measure 6" (15 cm) for standard-size, 7" (18 cm) for queen-size, and 8" (20.5 cm) for king-size sham. Press fold in place.

6) Refold fabric at pressed folds, right sides together, lapping short back piece over long back piece; pin.

7) Stitch ½" (1.3 cm) seam on the two long sides of the sham. Finish seams, using zigzag or overlock stitch.

8) Turn the pillow sham right side out; press. Insert the pillow.

Pillow Shams with Buttoned Flaps 🌙

Offering a sleek, contemporary look, this easy-to-sew pillow sham features a contrasting flap, embellished with buttons. This style of pillow sham is designed to fit a 26" (66 cm) square pillow, often called a European square pillow. The sham has a generous overlapping closure at the center back to conceal the pillow. The buttoned flap on the front is a mock opening, for decorative detailing.

✂ Cutting Directions

Cut one 27" (68.5 cm) square from fabric, for the pillow front. Cut two 20" × 27" (51 × 68.5 cm) rectangles from fabric, for the pillow back. Cut one 14" × 27" (35.5 × 68.5 cm) rectangle from contrasting fabric, for the pillow flap.

YOU WILL NEED

Two coordinating decorator fabrics.

Five ¾" (2 cm) buttons.

26" (66 cm) square pillow form.

How to Sew a Pillow Sham with a Buttoned Flap

1) Press ½" (1.3 cm), then 1½" (3.8 cm), to wrong side, along one long edge of rectangle for flap. Stitch close to inner fold.

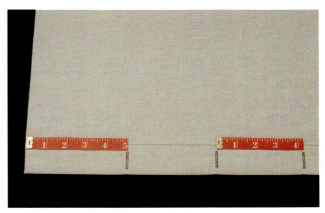

2) Mark buttonhole placement on hemmed edge of flap, 5" (12.5 cm) from each raw edge. Mark the placement of remaining buttonholes, spacing them 4¼" (10.8 cm) apart. Stitch vertical buttonholes at markings, centered on hemmed edge.

3) Place flap over pillow front, right sides up, matching raw edges at upper edge and sides. Mark placement for buttons; stitch buttons to pillow front. Reposition flap, and button over pillow front. Baste flap in place, ⅜" (1 cm) from raw edges.

4) Press ½" (1.3 cm), then 2" (5 cm), to wrong side, along one long edge of one pillow back piece. Stitch close to inner fold. Repeat for remaining back piece.

5) Position pillow back pieces over pillow front, right sides together, matching raw edges; hemmed edges overlap 8" (20.5 cm) at center. Pin in place.

6) Stitch ½" (1.3 cm) seam around the pillow sham. Trim the corners diagonally; finish seam allowances, using zigzag or overlock stitch. Turn right side out; insert pillow.

Decorative Sheet Flaps & Pillowcases ☀

Make a decorative sheet flap and a set of matching pillowcases from a plain, economical sheet and lace edging. The decorative sheet flap, which buttons onto a second top sheet, is designed to be folded down over the upper edge of the quilt or coverlet to provide a decorative finish along the upper edge of the bed.

This project uses two flat sheets. The upper edge of one sheet is used to make the decorative sheet flap, and the remainder of the sheet is used for the two pillowcases. The decorative sheet flap buttons onto the remaining top sheet to complete the set. Tucks and decorative trim embellish both the decorative sheet flap and the pillowcases.

54

Buttons and buttonholes secure the decorative sheet flap to the upper edge of the flat sheet.

✂ Cutting Directions

Cut the decorative sheet flap as on page 56, steps 1 and 2. From the remainder of the sheet, cut two pillowcases. The cut width of the fabric for each pillowcase is 40½" (103.3 cm); remove the side hems of the sheet, if necessary for width. The cut length of each pillowcase is 32" (81.5 cm) for a standard size, 36" (91.5 cm) for a queen size, and 42" (107 cm) for a king size; this allows for two tucks and seam allowances at each end.

How to Sew a Decorative Sheet Flap

1) Fold sheet over the upper edge of bedding to help determine the desired length of the sheet flap. Measure desired length of sheet flap, not including the width of the lace edging.

2) Add 11" (28 cm) for underlap, tucks, and seam allowances to the measurement determined in step 1. Cut sheet flap to this measurement; measure from upper hemmed edge of sheet. Hem of sheet will be at upper end of completed sheet flap.

3) Place rectangle for sheet flap, right side down, on ironing surface. With wrong sides of fabric together, press fold for tuck 10" (25.5 cm) from raw edge of fabric at lower edge of sheet flap.

4) Press second fold, 7" (18 cm) from raw edge, taking care not to press out fold for first tuck. Press third fold 4" (10 cm) from raw edge.

5) Stitch ¾" (2 cm) from fold to make tucks; for easier stitching, place tape on bed of sewing machine to use as a guide.

6) Press tucks toward raw edge of fabric. Press 1¼" (3.2 cm) on lower edge to wrong side.

7) Pin trim to lower edge, wrong sides together, with ends of trim extending ½" (1.3 cm) beyond side edges. Fold ends of trim under ¼" (6 mm) twice to wrong side. Stitch ¼" (6 mm) from raw edge of fabric. Press seam toward fabric. Hand-stitch or machine-stitch hems at ends of trim.

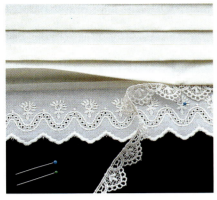

8) Lap pressed edge over the seam allowance on right side, encasing it; extend the pressed edge about ⅛" (3 mm) over the previous stitching. Stitch close to folded edge, inserting narrower lace trim under the fold, if desired.

9) Topstitch ⅜" (1 cm) from edge of lace, stitching through all layers.

10) Mark placement for buttonholes on upper hemmed edge of second top sheet, centering buttonholes on hem and spacing them about 12" (30.5 cm) apart. Stitch buttonholes.

11) Align top sheet and decorative sheet flap, wrong sides together, overlapping hemmed edges. Mark placement for buttons.

12) Stitch buttons to wrong side of decorative sheet flap on hemmed edge. Button decorative sheet flap onto top sheet.

How to Sew a Decorative Pillowcase

1) Press foldline 7" and 4" (18 and 10 cm) from 40½" (103.3 cm) edge of fabric. Stitch tucks and attach trim as in steps 5 to 9, opposite; cut ends of trim even with edge of fabric in step 7.

2) Fold fabric in half, right sides together, matching raw edges. Stitch ¼" (6 mm) from raw edges. Finish seams, using zigzag or overlock stitch. Turn pillowcase right side out.

Shower Curtains from Sheets

Shower curtains can be made easily from flat sheets. Many bed sheets have a decorative upper edge, such as a lace edging, ruffle, or printed border. Take advantage of the decorative edge by using it for one of two styles of shower curtains. Use the sheet upside down so the decorative edge becomes the lower edge of the shower curtain. Or make a shower curtain with a valance, using the decorative edge of the sheet for the lower edge of the valance.

For hanging the shower curtain, buttonholes or grommets can be applied along the upper edge. Attach the curtain to the shower bar with snap-on rings, shower curtain hooks, or lengths of grosgrain ribbon tied in bows.

A full-size sheet, measuring 81" × 96" (206 × 244 cm), can be used to make a standard 72" × 72" (183 × 183 cm) shower curtain.

✂ Cutting Directions

For a 72" × 72" (183 × 183 cm) shower curtain with attached valance, cut a full-size sheet to measure 76" (193 cm) wide. For a 12" (30.5 cm) valance, cut 14½" (36.8 cm) from the decorative upper edge of the sheet. For the curtain, cut the remaining sheet fabric to measure 78" (198 cm) long.

For a 72" × 72" (183 × 183 cm) shower curtain with decorative lower edge, cut a full-size sheet to measure 76" (193 cm) wide and 76" (193 cm) long, including the decorative border.

YOU WILL NEED

One full-size flat sheet with decorative edge.
Grommets and grommet attaching tool, optional.

Shower curtain with a decorative lower edge (above) is made from a sheet with a ruffled edging. The shower curtain with an attached valance (opposite) uses the printed border on the sheet to define the lower edge of the valance.

How to Sew a Shower Curtain with an Attached Valance from a Sheet

1) Fold under and stitch 3" (7.5 cm) double-fold hem on the lower edge of curtain panel. Fold under and stitch 1" (2.5 cm) double-fold hems on side edges of curtain and valance panels.

2) Press ½" (1.3 cm), then 2" (5 cm), to wrong side, at upper edge of valance.

3) Place valance on flat surface, wrong side up; open out hem. Place curtain panel, right side down, over valance panel, with upper edge of the curtain panel even with foldline of valance panel.

4) Refold valance, encasing upper edge of curtain panel; pin in place. Stitch close to inner fold.

5) Mark placement for 12 grommets or buttonholes ¾" (2 cm) from upper edge; place the end marks 1½" (3.8 cm) from the sides, and evenly space the remaining marks.

6) Fasten grommets (**a**) securely at markings, following manufacturer's directions. Or, for buttonholes, make ½" (1.3 cm) vertical buttonholes (**b**), aligning the upper edge of buttonholes with marks.

How to Sew a Shower Curtain with Decorative Lower Edge from a Sheet

1) Fold under and stitch 1" (2.5 cm) double-fold hem on each side of curtain panel.

2) Fold under and stitch 2" (5 cm) double-fold hem on upper edge of curtain panel. Finish as in steps 5 and 6, above.

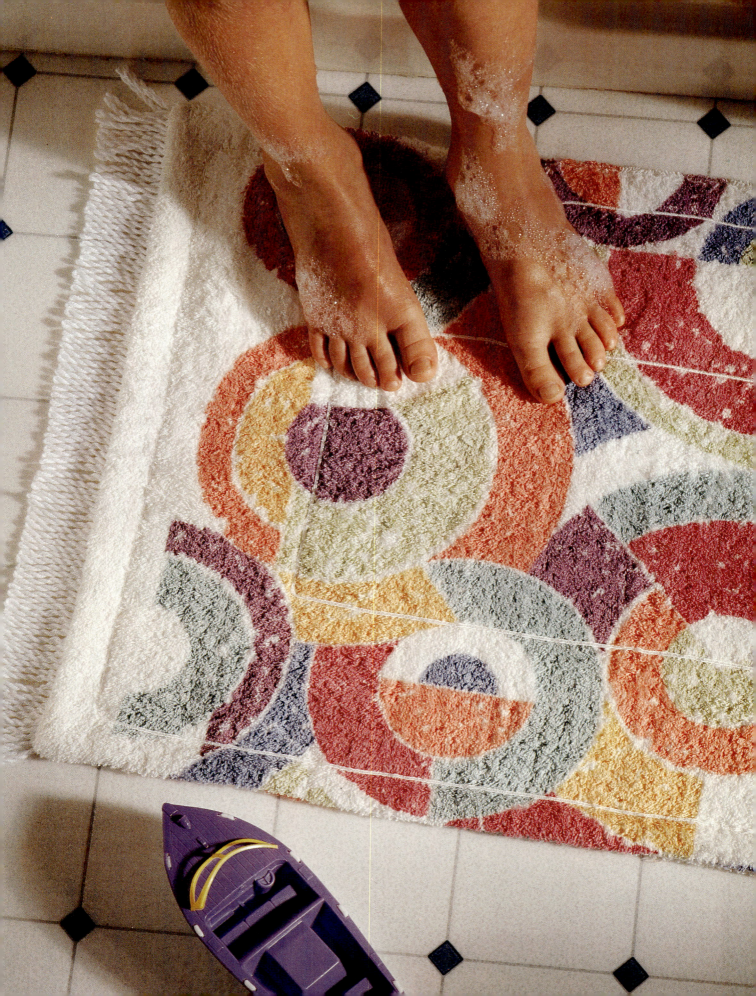

Terry Cloth Bath Mats 🌙

Comfortable, absorbent bath mats can be made from two layers of terry cloth, sewn together with cotton fringe at each end. For a decorative quilted effect, cotton cording or soutache braid is applied to the top of the mat by stitching through both layers, in a technique called *couching*. This technique uses wide zigzag or blanket stitches to secure the cording or soutache on each side of the trim.

Cording may be easily couched to the bath mat with the help of a cording foot. The trim is threaded through a hole in the foot and is guided automatically as you sew, leaving your hands free to turn the fabric. If a cording foot is not available, the trim can be stitched to the mat using a general-purpose foot and the zigzag stitch.

The bath mat can be made from either a loop or cut pile terry cloth. Choose fringe and cording or soutache braid that are colorfast. To prevent shrinkage, prewash the fabric and all trims.

✂ Cutting Directions

For the bath mat top and bottom, cut two rectangles of fabric 1" (2.5 cm) longer and wider than the desired finished length and width of the bath mat, excluding the length of the fringe. Cut each piece separately, rather than layered, for accuracy. Cut two lengths of fringe equal to the finished length of the short sides plus 1½" (3.8 cm).

YOU WILL NEED

Woven terry cloth fabric; knit or stretch fabric is not suitable.

Cotton fringe.

Cotton cording or soutache braid.

How to Sew a Terry Cloth Bath Mat

1) Pin fringe to right side of bath mat top on each short side, aligning upper edge of fringe tape with raw edge of fabric; fold up ¾" (2 cm) at the ends of fringe, and position folded ends ½" (1.3 cm) from the long edges of fabric. Baste in place.

2) Pin the bath mat top to the bath mat back, right sides together. Stitch ½" (1.3 cm) seam around mat, pivoting at corners; leave an opening for turning on one side. Avoid catching fringe in stitching.

3) Clip corners diagonally. Turn bath mat right side out. Slipstitch opening closed.

4) Mark a line 1" (2.5 cm) from each edge of mat. Mark a second set of lines 4" (10 cm) from the first set.

5) Hand-baste top to back within ¼" (6 mm) of each line, to prevent layers from shifting when you are couching.

6) **Align** cording foot with first line on mat. Place the cording or soutache braid from front to back through the hole in the foot. Set the machine for zigzag stitch, and set stitch width so stitches will catch fabric on both sides of cording or braid.

7) **Stitch** over cording, guiding fabric so the stitching follows marked line; cording will feed by itself. Pivot at corners, keeping needle down in fabric on the left side of the cording as you turn fabric. (Contrasting thread was used to show detail.)

8) **Stop** stitching about 2" (5 cm) from the starting point. Cut cording so end overlaps starting point about ½" (1.3 cm). Continue stitching, overlapping cording and stitching over both ends to secure.

9) **Repeat** steps 6 through 8 to couch the cording or soutache braid on second set of lines.

Gathered Wastebasket Cover 🌙

Dress up an inexpensive cylindrical wastebasket with a gathered fabric cover. An inner lining fits snugly against the wastebasket to hold the cover in place. In some cases, depending on the slope of the sides and the fabric used, you may want to use two small circles of self-adhesive hook and loop tape to hold the cover in place. For best results, choose a wastebasket with sides that are straight or nearly straight and an upper rim that does not curve outward. Washable fabric that has been prewashed will allow easy laundering of the cover.

✂ Cutting Directions

Cut a rectangle from lining fabric about 6" (15 cm) longer and wider than the height and the upper circumference of the wastebasket. Follow steps 1 to 3, opposite, for cutting the lining and bottom of the cover Cut a rectangle from the fabric for the outer cover with the length equal to twice the upper circumference of the wastebasket and the width equal to the height of the wastebasket plus 1⅜" (3.5 cm). Seam fabric widths together, if necessary.

YOU WILL NEED

Mediumweight fabric, for cover and lining.

Purchased welting.

Cylindrical wastebasket.

Circles of self-adhesive hook and loop tape, optional.

How to Sew a Gathered Wastebasket Cover

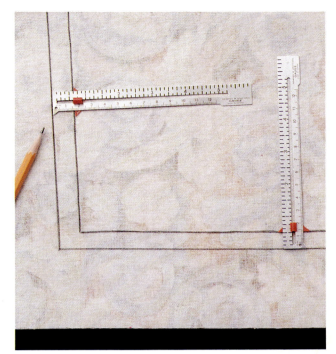

1) Place wastebasket on right side of lining rectangle; wrap fabric snugly around wastebasket, and pin in place in a straight line on back of wastebasket. Mark seamline as pinned, using a pencil; mark upper and lower edges of wastebasket.

2) Remove pins. Add 5⁄8" (1.5 cm) to upper edge and back edges to allow for 1⁄2" (1.3 cm) seam allowances and 1⁄8" (3 mm) for ease. Add a 1⁄2" (1.3 cm) seam allowance to lower edge. Cut on outside lines.

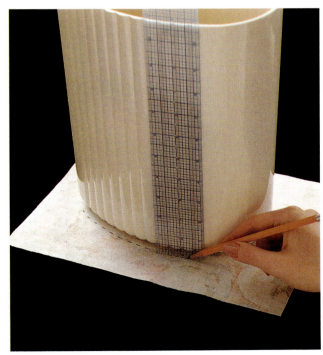

3) Cut a rectangle for outer cover, opposite; set aside. Trace around bottom of the wastebasket on wrong side of outer fabric, using a pencil and straightedge as shown. Add 1⁄2" (1.3 cm) seam allowance. Cut on outside line.

4) Fold the outer cover in half, right sides together; stitch 1⁄2" (1.3 cm) seam. Press seam open. Divide upper and lower edges of outer cover into fourths; mark, using seam as one mark. Repeat for lining.

(Continued on next page)

5) Zigzag over cord on wrong side of the outer cover, ⅜" (1 cm) from the raw edges; do not catch cord in stitching. Repeat at the lower edge, stitching on the right side.

6) Position stitching line of welting ½" (1.3 cm) from raw edge of fabric. Stitch welting to right side of lining at upper edge, using zipper foot; match raw edges and start 2" (5 cm) from end of welting.

7) Stop stitching 2" (5 cm) from point where ends of welting will meet. Cut off one end of the welting so it overlaps the other end by 1" (2.5 cm).

8) Remove stitching from one end of welting, and trim ends of cording so they just meet.

9) Fold under ½" (1.3 cm) of fabric on overlapping end. Lap it around the other end; finish stitching the welting to lining.

10) Pin the outer cover to lining on upper edge, right sides together, matching marks and seams. Pull up cord to gather; distribute gathers evenly, and pin.

11) Stitch a ½" (1.3 cm) seam, crowding cording. Turn the cover so right side of lining is on outside.

12) Repeat step 10 for lower edge, with wrong sides together. Stitch scant ½" (1.3 cm) from lower edge. Clip to stitching line at ½" (1.3 cm) intervals around lower edge.

13) Fold bottom piece into fourths; mark. Divide lower edge of gathered cover into fourths; mark, using seam as one mark. Pin bottom piece to cover, right sides together; match marks. Stitch ½" (1.3 cm) seam. Turn right side out, and insert wastebasket.

14) Position circles of self-adhesive hook and loop tape near upper edge to hold cover in place, if necessary; place hook tape on the wastebasket and loop tape on the fabric.

Reversible Seat Covers ☀

Freshen the look of dining-room and kitchen chairs with simple seat covers. The lined cover is shaped at the front of the chair and secured to the chair with fabric ties at the back legs. To make the seat cover reversible, use a coordinating decorator fabric for the lining. For best results, choose firmly woven, mediumweight decorator fabrics. These fabrics wear well and are easy to work with. When working with heavier fabrics, select a lighter-weight fabric for the lining. To add a decorative touch to the cover, embellish the lower edge with a contrasting trim, such as ribbon or braid. This seat cover is suitable for armless chairs that have open backs and smooth, flat seats.

✂ Cutting Directions

Make the seat cover pattern as on page 74. Cut one piece each from fabric and lining. Cut four fabric strips, 2" (5 cm) wide and 10" to 16" (25.5 to 40.5 cm) long, for ties.

YOU WILL NEED

Muslin, for pattern.

Decorator fabric.

Lining fabric.

Decorative trim, optional.

Seat covers can give an updated look to dining-room and kitchen chairs. Make the covers reversible by using a decorator fabric for the lining, and, for added interest, embellish the lower edge with a decorative trim.

How to Make a Seat Cover Pattern

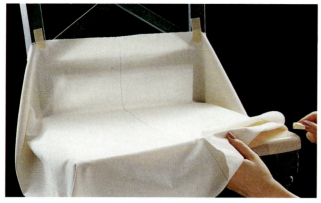

1) Measure chair seat, and add 3" to 4" (7.5 to 10 cm) on all sides for drop length; cut a piece of muslin about 4" (10 cm) larger than measurements. Mark center line, following lengthwise grain. Center muslin on seat; pin or tape in place.

2) Clip fabric diagonally at back corners, so fabric fits around the back posts; make additional clips as necessary for smooth fit.

3) Smooth fabric around sides and front of chair; pin out excess fabric at front corners. Mark seamline at front corners, using pencil.

4) Mark seamline around the back posts, using pencil. Pin-mark ends of seat cover on drop, at sides of chair; repeat for drop at chair back.

5) Pin-mark the lower edge of cover at the desired length around front, sides, and back; drop length on sides and back should align. Mark the seamlines.

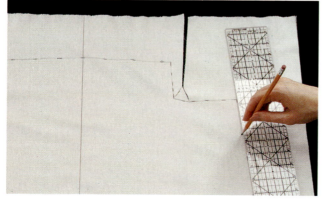

6) Remove muslin from the chair. Redraw seamlines as necessary, using straightedge; redraw any curved lines, drawing smooth curves. Reposition muslin on chair; make corrections, if necessary.

7) Add ½" (1.3 cm) seam allowances. Cut pattern on the marked lines.

How to Sew a Seat Cover

1) Press under ½" (1.3 cm) on one short end of the fabric strip for tie. Press the strip in half lengthwise, wrong sides together. Open, and press raw edges to the center crease, wrong sides together; refold at the original crease. Repeat for remaining fabric strips.

2) Stitch close to folded edges of strips. Pin one tie to right side of seat cover at lower back corner, with raw edges even and long stitched edge of tie ½" (1.3 cm) from lower edge of cover. Baste tie in place. Repeat for remaining ties.

3) Pin seam at front corners of seat cover; stitch. Repeat for lining. Press seams to one side, pressing seams of the seat cover and the lining in opposite directions.

4) Pin lining to the seat cover, right sides together and raw edges even. Stitch ½" (1.3 cm) seam, leaving 6" (15 cm) opening, centered on back of seat cover.

5) Trim outside corners diagonally; clip any curves and inside corners. Press seam allowances open.

6) Turn cover right side out; press. Slipstitch opening closed. Position trim, if desired, at the lower edge of the cover or lining, using glue stick. Turn under ½" (1.3 cm) at ends. Topstitch trim in place; stitch both sides in same direction to prevent diagonal wrinkles.

7) Position seat cover on chair; secure ties in bow or square knot.

Tablecloths & Placemats with Lace Edging 🌙

These tablecloths and placemats feature a border of flat lace edging softly gathered at each corner. Flat lace edging has one scalloped edge and one straight edge. It is available in a variety of styles and widths. Depending on the fabric and lace selected, the tablecloth or placemats can be either elegant or casual. Choose a lace that complements the fabric, such as a Battenberg lace border on a crisp, white linen fabric for a very elegant look. Or for a homespun look, use a cotton Cluny lace with a casual cotton check.

To determine the finished size of a tablecloth, measure the table and add twice the desired drop length, or overhang, to the length and width. An attractive drop length is about one-third the height of the table. Avoid seaming the fabric by choosing a fabric and a lace edging wide enough to achieve the desired finished width. If seaming is necessary, seam equal widths to each side of a center panel. Placemat sizes may vary. A good finished size, including the border, is 13" × 18" (33 × 46 cm).

✂ Cutting Directions

To determine the cut size of the fabric, subtract twice the width of the lace from the finished length and width of the tablecloth or placemat; add 1" (2.5 cm) to these measurements.

Cut the lace to a length equal to twice the finished length of the tablecloth plus twice the finished width of the tablecloth plus eight times the width of the lace.

YOU WILL NEED

Fabric, for tablecloth or placemats.
Flat lace edging, 2" to 5" (5 to 12.5 cm) wide.

Placemats (above) with ornate lace edging have a romantic look. The tablecloth (opposite) uses a proportionately wider lace trim.

How to Sew a Tablecloth or Placemat with Lace Edging

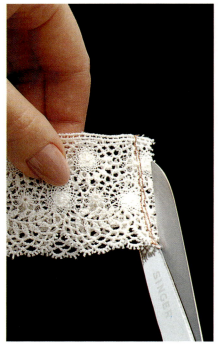

1) Sew cut ends of lace together in 1/4" (6 mm) seam, using short stitch length. Stitch again close to first stitching. Trim the seam allowances close to stitching; press to one side.

2) Measure a distance from seam in lace that is half the cut length of fabric plus 2½" (6.5 cm); pin-mark. Starting at pin mark, divide lace circle into fourths, and pin-mark.

3) Mark the fabric at the center of each side. Also mark points on each side 2½" (6.5 cm) from corners.

4) Pin or tape the lace to fabric, right sides together; match pin marks on lace to center marks on fabric, and position straight edge of lace ½" (1.3 cm) from raw edges. Pin or tape from center marks to marks near corners, leaving extra lace free at corners.

5) Sew hand running stitches for gathering, along the straight edge of lace between corner markings.

6) Pull gathering thread so lace fits fabric at corner; distribute gathers evenly. Pin or tape in place; secure gathering thread.

7) Repeat steps 5 and 6 for remaining three corners. Stitch along the straight edge of lace, using a narrow zigzag stitch; stitch through the tape, if used. Pivot at the corners.

8) Remove tape, if used. Remove gathering threads. On wrong side, press excess fabric away from lace.

9) Stitch along pressed fold, on the right side of the placemat, using a zigzag stitch.

10) Trim fabric close to stitching on the wrong side.

Two-way Table Runner 🌙

This two-way table runner has a unique design and can serve as placemats for a seating of four. Although it may look complicated, the ends are cut at 45° angles, so they are easily joined at the center. Many quilter's rulers have guidelines for cutting 45° angles. Or, to make a good substitute for a quilter's 45° angle, fold a square piece of paper in half diagonally.

An interesting effect can be created with this runner by using a striped fabric, although this requires matching. To use a stripe successfully, you need an even stripe, one that has a center stripe with identical spacing and colors on each side. Cut the table runner pieces so the stripes are identical across the width of each piece, positioning an obvious stripe in the center.

Solid-colored decorator fabrics or those with small all-over prints also work well for this runner. A fabric with a large dominant motif may not be as attractive when cut and mitered in the center. The amount of fabric needed varies with the width of the fabric and the size of the table.

The entire runner is lined, eliminating the need for hems. If desired, the runner can be lined with another decorator fabric to make it reversible.

✂ Cutting Directions

Measure the length of the table and add 16" (40.5 cm) to allow for an 8" (20.5 cm) drop, or overhang, on each end of the table. Also add 3" (7.5 cm) for seam allowances. Divide this measurement in half to determine the cut length of the two pieces that will be used for the lengthwise direction of the table runner. Repeat this procedure to determine the cut length of the two rectangles that will be used for the crosswise direction of the table runner. The cut width of all pieces is equal to 17" (43 cm). This width allows for ½" (1.3 cm) seam allowances on the sides. Cut four backing pieces from lining or fabric, to the same size as the table runner top pieces. The ends of the pieces are angled in step 1, page 82.

YOU WILL NEED

Decorator fabric, for table runner top.
Lining fabric or decorator fabric, for backing.

How to Sew a Two-way Table Runner

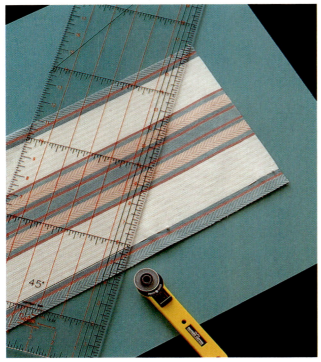

1) Fold one fabric rectangle in half lengthwise. Using quilter's ruler, cut each end at 45° angle from end of fold to sides. Repeat for remaining three pieces and all lining pieces.

2) Place crosswise runner piece over lengthwise runner piece, right sides together; pin along one angled edge. Repeat with remaining two pieces.

3) Stitch ½" (1.3 cm) seam from outer edge to point along pinned side. Begin stitching ½" (1.3 cm) from the outer edge; backstitch at beginning. Repeat for remaining two pieces.

4) Press seams open. Pin pieced sections right sides together, matching seams at center of runner.

5) Stitch, beginning and ending with backstitch, ½" (1.3 cm) from edges. Press seam open.

6) Repeat steps 2 to 5 for lining. Pin lining to runner top, right sides together, matching seams and raw edges. Stitch, pivoting at inner and outer corners; leave an opening for turning along one long side.

7) Trim the outside corners across points; taper seam allowances at center point. Press seams open.

8) Turn the runner right side out. Press around outer edge. Slipstitch opening closed.

Round Tablecloths with Twisted Welting 🌙

A round tablecloth, puddled on the floor, adds an elegant decorator look to a room. Twisted welting at the edge of the tablecloth eliminates hemming and provides a decorative edge finish.

For best results, choose a soft, drapable fabric. To save time, choose solid-colored fabrics or small random prints that do not require matching. Avoid patterns with one-way designs.

Determine the diameter of the tablecloth by measuring the diameter of the table and adding twice the drop length; also add 6" (15 cm) to this measurement for puddling the fabric on the floor.

Two lengths of fabric are used to make this tablecloth. To determine the amount of fabric needed for the tablecloth, multiply the diameter of the tablecloth by two and divide by 36" (91.5 cm) to find the total yards (meters). Add about 2" (5 cm) to the total yardage needed for easier cutting. If you are using a patterned fabric, additional yardage may also be needed in order to match repeats. Use one full width of the fabric for the center of the tablecloth, and seam equal partial widths of fabric on each side.

To determine the welting yardage, multiply the diameter of the tablecloth by three and one-quarter and divide by 36" (91.5 cm). Add to this measurement about 6" (15 cm) for finishing the ends of the welting. The right side of the twisted welting can be easily identified, since it is the side where the inner edge of the tape is not visible. If the twisted welting you purchased twists in the opposite direction from the welting shown, transpose the words "left" and "right" in steps 6 to 8.

✂ Cutting Directions

Seam the fabric widths together and cut the tablecloth from the seamed panels as in steps 1 and 2, below.

YOU WILL NEED

54" (137 cm) decorator fabric.
Twisted welting.

How to Sew a Round Tablecloth with Twisted Welting

1) **Seam** side panels to the center panel, right sides together, using the selvage width as the seam allowance; match patterned fabrics, if necessary, as on page 39. Press seams open. Trim edge of selvage, if desired.

2) **Fold** fabric in half lengthwise, then crosswise. Pin the layers together to prevent them from slipping. Using a straightedge and pencil, mark an arc on fabric, measuring one-half the diameter of the tablecloth from folded center of fabric. (Marked line was exaggerated to show detail.)

(Continued on next page)

3) Cut the fabric on the marked line; remove pins.

4) Stitch twisted welting to tablecloth, right sides together, using zipper foot; align the outer edge of the welting tape to the raw edge of the fabric. Leave 1½" (3.8 cm) unstitched between the ends; leave 3" (7.5 cm) tails.

5) Remove the stitching from the welting tape on tails. Separate cords; wrap transparent tape around ends to prevent raveling.

6) Trim welting tape to 1" (2.5 cm) from stitching; overlap the ends and secure with transparent tape. Arrange cords so those at right turn up and those at left turn down.

7) Insert cords at the right end under welting tape, twisting and pulling them down until the welting is returned to its original shape. Secure in place, using transparent tape or pins.

8) Twist and pull cords at left end over cords at right end until twisted ends look like continuous twisted welting; check both sides of welting.

9) Stitch through all layers, using zipper foot, to secure the welting at the seamline; cords may be hand-basted or taped in place, if desired.

10) Finish the seam allowance, using zigzag stitch or overlock stitch. Trim ends of cords, if necessary, and apply liquid fray preventer to cut ends. Turn under the seam allowance, and edgestitch, using zipper foot.

Ruffled Table Covers

Create a ruffled table cover for a sofa table or night stand. These table covers can give a new look to older tables and provide the perfect opportunity to coordinate fabrics. For an attractive look, make the ruffled skirt about 10" (25 cm) long; shorter skirts have a tendency to flare out. To hold the table cover in place, concealed twill tape ties are used either under the table or around the table legs. This table cover may be combined with a glass top, if desired. Glass tabletops with polished edges are available in several sizes from many furniture retailers. Glass tabletops are also custom-cut by glass retailers.

✂ Cutting Directions

Make the pattern for the top of the tablecloth as on page 90, steps 1 and 2. Cut one top piece each from fabric, lining, and interfacing. Cut the skirt from fabric, with the length of the skirt equal to twice the desired length plus 1" (2.5 cm), to allow for ½" (1.3 cm) seam allowances. The cut width of the skirt is equal to one and one-half to two times the measurement around the tabletop plus 1" (2.5 cm) for seam allowances. If it is necessary to piece fabric widths together, also add 1" (2.5 cm) for each seam.

YOU WILL NEED

Decorator fabric.
Lining fabric.
Heavyweight sew-in interfacing.
Twill tape, for the ties.

How to Make a Ruffled Table Cover

1) Place a sheet of paper or interfacing on top of the table; draw pattern by marking the edge of the table, using a pencil.

2) Add ½" (1.3 cm) seam allowance to the pattern. Mark edge of pattern on center of each side. Cut fabric, lining, and interfacing pieces as on page 88.

3) Layer the fabric and lining top pieces, wrong sides together, with the interfacing between the layers; pin. Stitch the layers together around all sides, a scant ½" (1.3 cm) from edges. Trim the interfacing close to stitching. Pin-mark top piece on center of each side.

4) Stitch short ends of skirt together in ½" (1.3 cm) seam. Fold the skirt in half lengthwise, wrong sides together; press. Divide upper edge of the strip into fourths; pin-mark.

5) Zigzag over cording, a scant ½" (1.3 cm) from raw edge, leaving long cord tails; periodically stop stitching, with needle down, and pull on cording to gather fabric behind needle.

6) Pin the skirt to the top piece, right sides together, matching pin marks and distributing gathers evenly. Stitch ½" (1.3 cm) seam. Finish seam allowances, using zigzag stitch or overlock stitch.

7) Position table cover on table. Mark placement for ties to be secured underneath table or around legs.

8) Cut a strip of twill tape for each tie; stitch the ties in place along seamline at markings. Place the table cover on the table; secure ties.

Lamp Shade Covers 🌙

Convert a simple lamp shade into an attractive room accessory with a fabric lamp shade cover. Elastic at the upper and lower edges ensures that the shade cover fits snugly on the shade. The lower edge of the cover can be trimmed with either a self-fabric ruffle or a flat lace edging. The trim around the lower edge and the ruffled heading created by the elastic at the upper edge soften the shade, giving it a romantic look.

This shade cover is most suited to a lamp shade that measures 8" to 12" (20.5 to 30.5 cm) high and up to 42" (107 cm) in circumference at the lower edge. For best results, choose a lightweight fabric, such as cotton batiste or semisheer linen. Before beginning the project, drape the fabric over the shade with the light turned on, to test the effect the light may have on the color of the fabric.

✂ Cutting Directions

Cut a rectangle from the fabric, with the length equal to the lower circumference of the lamp shade plus 1½" (3.8 cm). The width of the rectangle is equal to the height of the shade plus 4" (10 cm).

For a self-fabric ruffle, cut a strip from fabric, 5" (12.5 cm) wide, with the length of the strip equal to twice the circumference of the lower edge of the shade. Piece the fabric strips as necessary for length.

YOU WILL NEED

¾ yd. to 1 yd. (0.7 m to 0.95 m) lightweight fabric, depending on size of shade and whether self-fabric ruffle is used.

¼" (6 mm) elastic, length equal to total distance around upper and lower edges of shade.

Flat lace edging, length equal to lower circumference of shade plus 2" (5 cm), for lace-trimmed shade.

Ribbon or cording, optional.

How to Sew a Lamp Shade Cover

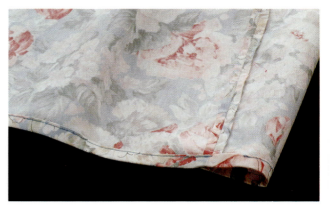

Lamp shade cover with self-fabric ruffle. 1) Stitch short ends of fabric rectangle together in ¼" (6 mm) seam; press seam open.

2) Press ¼" (6 mm), then ⅜" (1 cm), to wrong side, at lower edge. Stitch close to inner fold to form casing; leave 1" (2.5 cm) opening for inserting elastic.

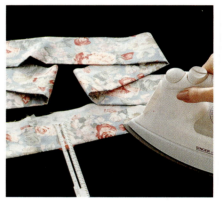

3) Press ¼" (6 mm), then 1¼" (3.2 cm), to wrong side, at upper edge. Stitch close to inner fold; leave a 1" (2.5 cm) opening for inserting elastic.

4) Stitch ⅜" (1 cm) from the first stitching at upper edge, to make a casing for elastic.

5) Stitch short ends of ruffle strip together in a ¼" (6 mm) seam; press seam open. Press 2" (5 cm) to wrong side at lower edge of strip.

6) Press 1" (2.5 cm) to the wrong side at upper edge of ruffle strip, overlapping upper and lower raw edges of strip.

7) Stitch two rows of long straight stitches, ⅝" (1.5 cm) and ⅞" (2.2 cm) from the upper edge of folded ruffle strip.

8) Divide ruffle strip and lower edge of shade cover into fourths; pin-mark. Pin ruffle, right side up, to right side of cover at pin marks; place lower edge of ruffle ⅛" (3 mm) above stitching line for lower casing.

9) **Pull** threads on ruffle strip, gathering strip to fit shade cover; distribute gathers evenly, and pin. Stitch between rows of gathering threads to secure ruffle to shade cover; remove gathering threads.

10) **Insert** elastic into upper and lower casings, using bodkin or safety pin; secure the ends together with a safety pin.

11) **Place** shade cover over shade, aligning top of casing with upper edge of shade; pull elastic at lower edge to underside of lamp shade, about 1" (2.5 cm).

12) **Adjust** the elastic for a snug fit. Remove shade cover. Overlap ends of the elastic, and stitch to secure. Ease ends of elastic into casings; stitch openings of casings closed.

13) **Arrange** shade cover on shade. Tie ribbon or cording around the top of the shade cover, if desired.

Lamp shade cover with flat lace edging. 1) Follow steps 1 to 4, opposite. Pin lace edging to shade cover so upper edge of lace is 1¼" (3.2 cm) above lower edge of cover. Fold under ½" (1.3 cm) at each end of lace, and butt ends at seam of cover.

2) **Stitch** along the upper edge of lace, using narrow zigzag stitch. Hand-stitch the ends of lace together. Complete the shade cover as in steps 10 to 13, above. (Contrasting thread was used to show detail.)

Finishing Touches

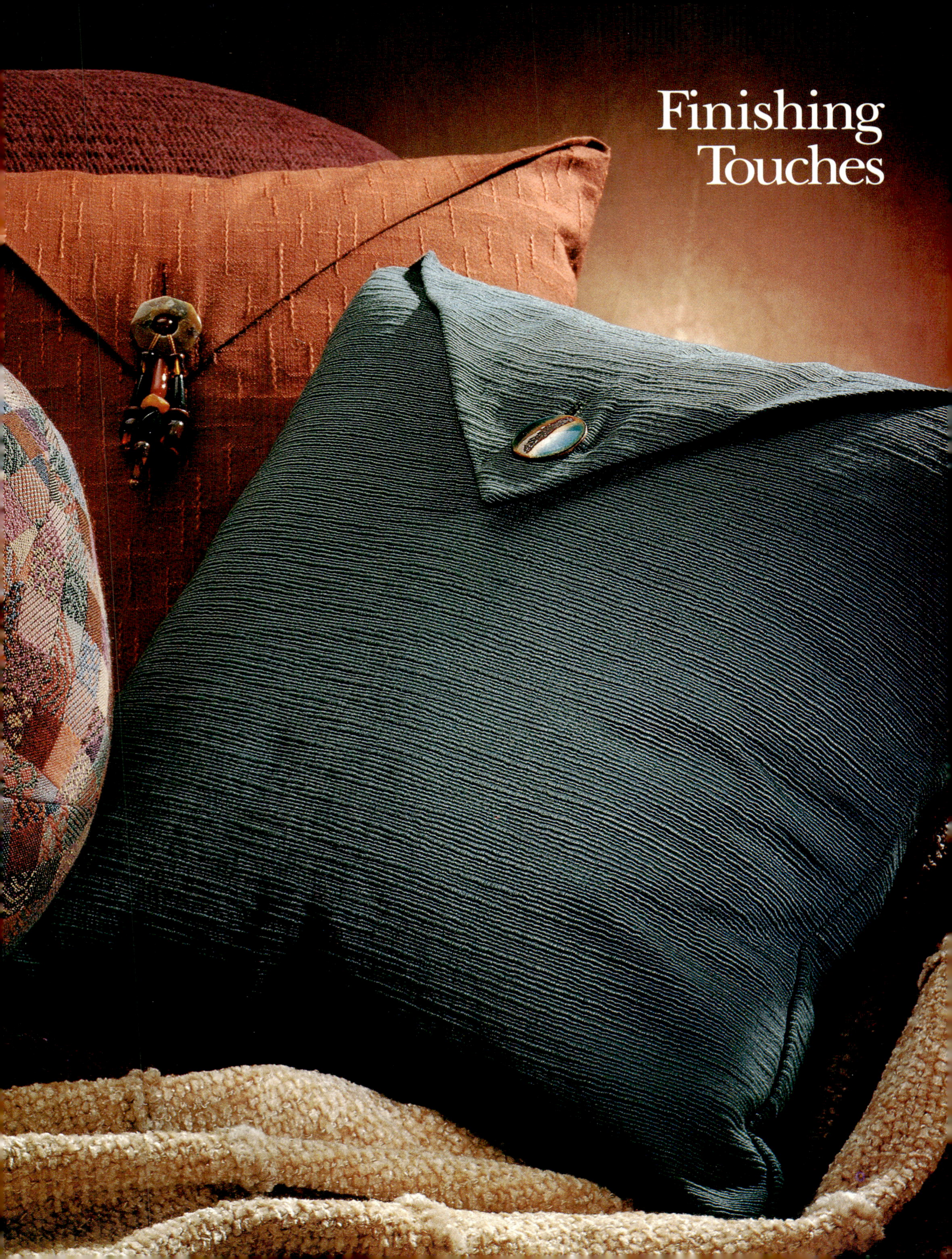

Bordered Pillows ☽

Make an eye-catching pillow by framing a center panel with a border and contrasting or coordinating corner pieces. For the center of the pillow front, choose a dominant motif from a decorator fabric or use a design from a preprinted fabric panel. Select fabrics for the side borders and corner pieces that emphasize the colors in the center panel. Or cut the corner pieces from the same fabric as the center panel to repeat the print. A large pillow form, 18" to 26" (46 to 66 cm) square, is recommended for this pillow. For best results, the center panel should measure about two-thirds of the pillow form. On 18" to 26" (46 to 66 cm) pillows, insets generally range from 12" to 17" (30.5 to 43 cm), with borders from 3" to 5" (7.5 to 12.5 cm).

✂ Cutting Directions

Cut the center panel of the pillow cover to the desired finished size plus 1" (2.5 cm), to allow for ½" (1.3 cm) seam allowances. Cut four border strips the same length as the cut size of the center panel; the cut width is equal to the desired finished width plus 1" (2.5 cm) for ½" (1.3 cm) seam allowances. Cut four squares for the corner pieces, with the sides equal to the cut width of the border strips. The pillow back is cut in step 4, below.

How to Sew a Bordered Pillow

1) Pin one border strip to upper edge of center panel, with right sides together and raw edges even; stitch ½" (1.3 cm) seam. Repeat for border strip on lower edge. Press seam allowances toward borders.

2) Stitch corner pieces to the ends of remaining border strips in ½" (1.3 cm) seams; these are the side border strips. Press seam allowances toward border strips.

3) Pin one side border strip to one unbordered side of center panel, with right sides together and raw edges even; stich a ½" (1.3 cm) seam. Repeat for remaining side.

4) Press seam allowances toward borders. Cut pillow cover back to size of pieced front. Pin the pillow cover front to pillow cover back, right sides together, matching raw edges and corners.

5) Stitch around the pillow cover in a ½" (1.3 cm) seam; leave an opening on one side for turning the pillow cover right side out and inserting pillow form. Trim corners diagonally. Press seams open.

6) Turn pillow cover right side out; insert pillow form. Slipstitch the opening closed.

Pillows with Knotted Ties ☽

These easy knife-edge pillows get their style from the knotted ties at the corners. For contrast, select a fabric for the ties that coordinates with the pillow fabric. Square or rectangular pillow forms of any size can be used.

✄ Cutting Directions

Cut one pillow front and one pillow back from fabric, with the length and width 1" (2.5 cm) larger than the pillow form. Make the pattern for the ties as in step 1, below. Cut four ties each from pillow fabric and contrasting fabric.

YOU WILL NEED

Decorator fabric, yardage depending on size of pillow; allow extra yardage for ties.

½ yd. (0.5 m) contrasting fabric, for ties.

Pillow form.

How to Sew a Pillow with Knotted Ties

1) Trace the partial pattern for ties (page 103) onto tracing paper; fold paper on the dotted line. Cut on solid lines; open full-size pattern. Cut pillow front, pillow back, and ties, above.

2) Place one tie piece from pillow fabric and one from contrasting fabric right sides together. Stitch ¼" (6 mm) seam, leaving 2" (5 cm) opening on one side. Trim seam allowances to ⅛" (3 mm) along stitching. Turn right side out; press. Slipstitch or edgestitch opening closed. Repeat for remaining ties.

(Continued on next page)

3) Mark a line through center of each tie. Place a tie on right side of pillow top at each corner, as shown, with marked line of tie a scant 5/8" (1.5 cm) from raw edges of fabric.

4) Stitch across ties on marked lines, backstitching at ends. Fold ties and pin to pillow top, to prevent catching them in the stitching when pillow cover is sewn.

6) Press seam allowances open. Hand-gather fabric along stitching line for tie at each corner; secure with wrapped thread or rubber bands.

7) Turn pillow cover right side out. Insert pillow form. Slipstitch opening closed.

5) Place pillow front and pillow back right sides together, matching raw edges. Stitch a ½" (1.3 cm) seam around pillow cover, leaving opening on one side.

8) Make single knot in each tie; fan out ends.

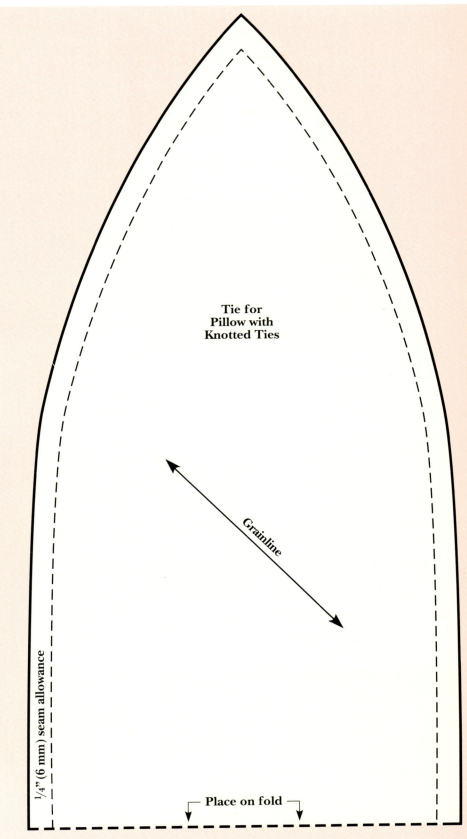

Tie for
Pillow with
Knotted Ties

Grainline

¼" (6 mm) seam allowance

⌐ **Place on fold** ¬

Envelope Pillows ☽

This decorative envelope pillow cover is created from a rectangle of fabric that is stitched at one end to produce a triangular flap. The envelope flap is held in place with a decorative button or beads. The pillow cover also has an inner hidden flap to keep the pillow form tucked neatly in place. The rectangle can be cut on either the crosswise or the lengthwise grain of the fabric. Decorator fabric that measures 54" (137 cm) wide may be used for a square pillow up to 18" (46 cm), cut on the crosswise grain of the fabric. For a larger pillow, cut the rectangle on the lengthwise grain.

✂ Cutting Directions

Cut one fabric rectangle, with the length of the rectangle equal to two and one-half times the size of the pillow form plus 6½" (16.3 cm). The width of the fabric rectangle is equal to the size of the pillow form plus 2" (5 cm) for two 1" (2.5 cm) seam allowances.

How to Sew an Envelope Pillow

1) **Finish** edge of one short end of rectangle, using zigzag or overlock stitch. Fold 6" (15 cm) to wrong side and press fold, for rectangular inner flap.

2) **Fold** rectangle in half lengthwise, right sides together, matching raw edges. Stitch ½" (1.3 cm) seam on short end opposite the end with rectangular flap.

3) **Press** the seam open to a point; trim the point.

4) **Turn** stitched end right side out, centering seam to make triangular flap. Press diagonal edges. Finish lower edge of flap facing.

5) **Stitch** facing of triangular flap in place 1" (2.5 cm) from lower edge through both layers. Fold flap down along stitching line; press.

6) Fold fabric in half, right sides together, aligning fold of rectangular flap with fold of triangular flap.

7) Refold the rectangular flap to the opposite side, enclosing triangular flap. Pin the raw edges together along both sides.

8) Stitch 1" (2.5 cm) seams on both sides of the pillow cover. Trim to ½" (1.3 cm). Turn right side out so rectangular flap is on the inside, triangular flap is on the outside.

9) Mark placement of button and buttonhole. Make buttonhole and sew on button, keeping rectangular inner flap free.

10) Insert the pillow form, tucking it under the rectangular inner flap. Button the triangular flap.

Sphere Pillows

Add a dimensional sphere pillow to a grouping of pillows, for a unique accent. The 12" (30.5 cm) pillow is constructed from six wedge-shaped fabric pieces. Make the pillow from a single fabric or use a second color for alternating wedge pieces. Use firmly woven fabrics, and avoid fabrics with high sheen.

For professional results, stuff the pillow very firmly. This fills out the seams, preventing a puckered look. Purchase a good-quality polyester fiberfill so it will not become lumpy when compacted.

Stitch pieces together, taking care to stitch accurate ½" (1.3 cm) seams, and use a short stitch length, about 10 to 12 stitches per inch (2.5 cm).

✂ Cutting Directions

Make the pattern as in step 1, below. Cut six pieces from fabric.

YOU WILL NEED

⅔ yd. (0.63 m) decorator fabric, in one or two colors.

Polyester fiberfill, about 32 oz. (1 kg).

Autograph pillow is made from two fabrics, in school colors. The pillow is signed with a permanent-ink marking pen.

How to Sew a Sphere Pillow

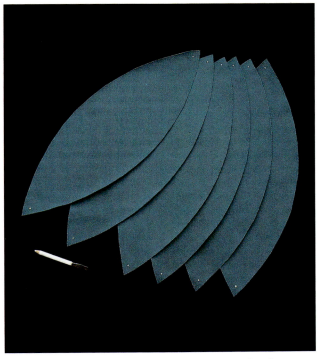

1) Trace the partial pattern (page 111) onto tracing paper. Fold paper on dotted line; cut on solid lines. Transfer dot at point to the opposite end of pattern. Open full-size pattern.

2) Cut the pillow pieces on the bias; transfer dot to wrong side of each piece, using pencil or chalk.

(Continued on next page)

3) Align two pillow pieces, right sides together, matching dots. Stitch from upper dot exactly to lower dot, using ½" (1.3 cm) seam allowance and short stitch length; backstitch at ends. Finger-press seam open. Repeat to stitch three two-piece sections.

4) Align two pillow sections, right sides together, matching dots; stitch ½" (1.3 cm) seam. Repeat for the remaining section; leave 4" to 6" (10 to 15 cm) opening near one end of the last seam.

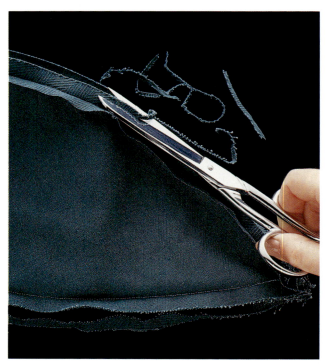

5) Trim the seam allowances to ⅜" (1 cm), if desired; this reduces bulk of heavier fabrics. Do not clip the seam allowances, to avoid weakening seams. Turn pillow right side out.

6) Stuff pillow firmly with polyester fiberfill. Compact stuffing periodically, using blunt instrument, such as a wooden spoon. Pin opening closed; slipstitch.

Pattern for a Sphere Pillow

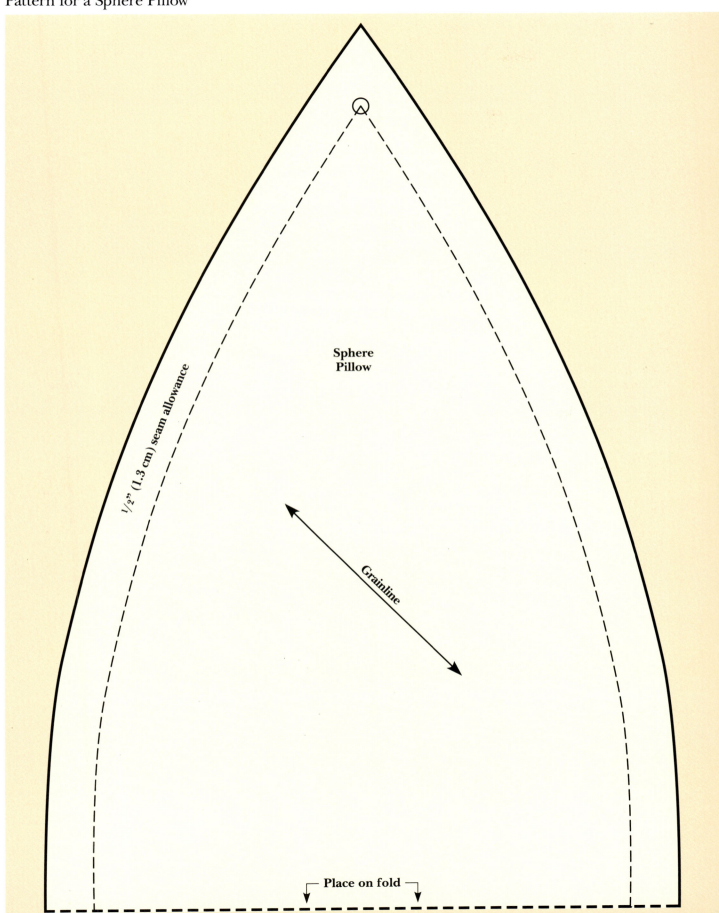

½" (1.3 cm) seam allowance

Sphere
Pillow

Grainline

Place on fold

Fringed Pillows ◗

This no-sew pillow is created by simply raveling the edges of two fabric squares and tying the fringe together over the pillow form. The fringe can be knotted in a single row around the pillow, or in multiple rows for a heavier effect. The finished length of the fringe may range from 3" to 7" (7.5 to 18 cm), depending on the look desired.

For best results, select fabrics that ravel easily. Loosely woven casement fabrics work especially well. When working with white or off-white fabric, a white pillow form may be used. For colored fabrics, where the white pillow form would show through, you may want to substitute a simple knife-edge pillow in a color that blends with the fabric.

✄ Cutting Directions

Cut two fabric squares 12" to 20" (30.5 to 51 cm) larger than the pillow form, cutting the fabric exactly on the grainline. It may be helpful to pull the lengthwise and crosswise threads at the desired measurements and cut along the pulled threads.

YOU WILL NEED

Fabric that ravels easily.

Pillow form or purchased knife-edge pillow in a color that blends with fabric.

How to Make a Fringed Pillow

1) Remove threads, two or three at a time, along each edge of fabric piece until center woven area is 1/8" (3 mm) larger than pillow form. Repeat for remaining fabric piece.

2) Center the pillow form on wrong side of one fabric piece. Position remaining fabric piece, wrong side down, over pillow form; align lengthwise threads of top piece with crosswise threads of bottom piece.

3) Tie the threads from each fabric piece in a knot, starting at one corner, and working in clusters of about 1/2" (1.3 cm). Check periodically to make sure edges of fabric remain aligned at corners.

4) Tie second row of knots about 1/2" (1.3 cm) below first row, if desired, by using thread clusters from the adjacent knots, as shown. Repeat for third or fourth row of knots, if desired. Trim fringe to desired length.

Beanbag Chairs ✺

For lounging in front of the television or curling up to read a book, use this comfortable beanbag chair. Although the name implies that the bag is filled with beans, it is actually filled with polystyrene pellets, making the chair lightweight and moldable. Beanbag chairs can be made in either a child size or an adult size.

For added durability, the beanbag chair consists of a muslin inner lining, which holds the pellets, and an outer cover. The inner lining is zippered for convenience in filling the bag. The outer cover is also zippered, making it easy to remove for laundering or dry cleaning. For the outer cover, select a mediumweight fabric, such as wide-wale corduroy, denim, canvas, or upholstery fabric.

✄ Cutting Directions

For the adult-size beanbag chair, make the pattern for the side pieces as in step 1 below; cut six side pieces from fabric and six side pieces from lining. For the top of the chair, cut one circle each from the fabric and the lining, with the radius equal to 5½" (14 cm). For the bottom of the chair, make the pattern as in steps 2 and 3 below; cut two pieces each from the fabric and the lining.

For the child-size chair, make the pattern for the side pieces as in step 1 below; cut six side pieces from fabric and six side pieces from lining. For the

top of the chair, cut one circle each from the fabric and the lining, with the radius equal to 4½" (11.5 cm). For the bottom of the chair, make the pattern as in steps 2 and 3 below; cut two pieces each from the fabric and the lining.

YOU WILL NEED

For adult-size chair:

5 yd. (4.6 m) mediumweight to heavyweight fabric, 45" to 48" (115 to 122 cm) wide. Or 3½ yd. (3.2 m) of 54" to 60" (137 to 152.5 cm) fabric.

Muslin, for inner lining, yardage same as for outer cover.

Zipper, 22" (56 cm) long.

Polystyrene pellets, approximately 6 cu. ft. (1.85 cu. m).

1" (2.5 cm) grid, such as cutting mat or graph paper.

For child-size chair:

3 yd. (2.75 m) mediumweight to heavyweight fabric, 45" to 48" (115 to 122 cm) wide. Or 2½ yd. (2.3 m) of 54" to 60" (137 to 152.5 cm) fabric.

Muslin, for inner lining, yardage same as for outer cover.

Zipper, 18" (46 cm) long.

Polystyrene pellets, approximately 4 cu. ft. (1.27 cu. m).

1" (2.5 cm) grid, such as cutting mat or graph paper.

How to Sew a Beanbag Chair

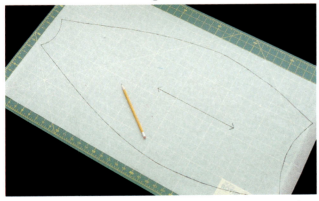

1) Place tracing paper over a 1" (2.5 cm) grid. Make full-size pattern for sides of chair, using the diagram on page 117 as a guide. Cut side pieces from fabric and lining.

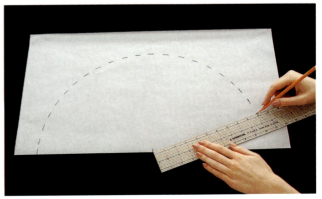

2) Fold paper in half; make a mark at center of fold. Using straightedge and pencil, mark arc on paper measuring 10" (25.5 cm) from the marked point for child-size chair or 12" (30.5 cm) from marked point for adult-size chair. Cut on marked line.

(Continued on next page)

3) Unfold paper; mark a line ½" (1.3 cm) from fold. Cut on marked line, and discard smallest piece of circle; remainder of circle is pattern for bottom of chair. Cut chair bottom pieces from fabric and lining as on page 115.

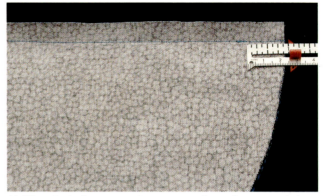

4) Pin chair bottom pieces together along straight edges. Machine-baste a ½" (1.3 cm) seam; using a regular stitch length, stitch at the ends of seam for 1" (2.5 cm). Press seam open.

5) Center zipper right side down over seam allowances, with zipper teeth on seamline. Glue-baste in place, using glue stick. Stitch down each side of zipper tape ¼" (6 mm) from zipper teeth.

6) Stitch long edges of side pieces, right sides together, in ½" (1.3 cm) seam; leave last seam unstitched. Press seam allowances to one side, pressing all in same direction.

7) Topstitch ⅜" (1 cm) from seams. Stitch remaining seam; press seam allowances to one side, and topstitch.

8) Staystitch upper edge of bag a scant ½" (1.3 cm) from edge. From raw edge, clip seam allowance at ½" (1.3 cm) intervals.

9) Divide the outer edge of top circle into six parts; mark. Pin the upper edge of bag to top circle, right sides together, matching seams of sides to marks on circle. Stitch ½" (1.3 cm) seam.

10) Press seam allowances toward the bag sides; topstitch ⅜" (1 cm) from the seam. Repeat steps 8 and 9 for the bag bottom, leaving zipper partially opened.

11) Turn bag right side out through the zipper opening. Press the bottom seam allowances toward bag sides; topstitch ⅜" (1 cm) from seam.

12) Repeat steps 4 to 11 for inner lining. Insert the lining into outer cover; fill the bag with polystyrene pellets. Close zippers.

Diagram for the Side Patterns of the Adult-size and Child-size Beanbag Chairs

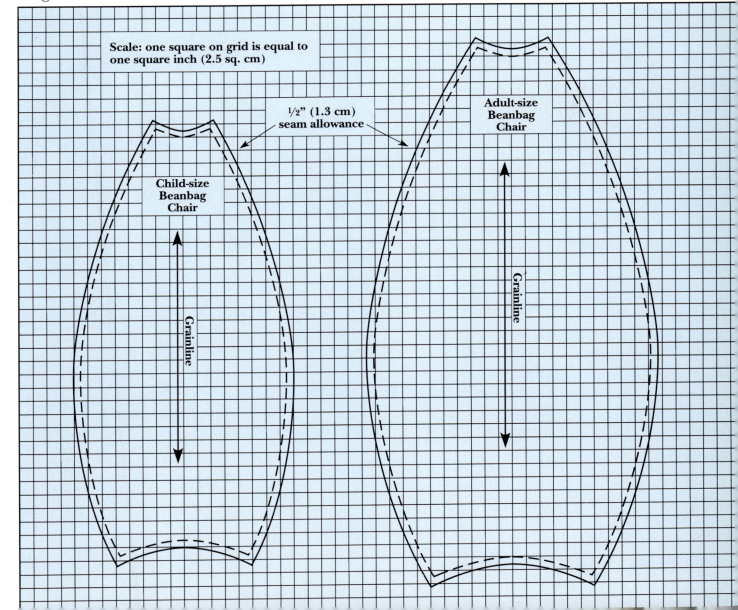

Scale: one square on grid is equal to one square inch (2.5 sq. cm)

½" (1.3 cm) seam allowance

Adult-size Beanbag Chair

Child-size Beanbag Chair

Grainline

Synthetic Fur Throws 🌙

Create a warm, luxurious throw from synthetic fur and a fringe trim. Line the throw using a stable knit fabric with a soft, brushed nap, giving the appearance of suede. For an elegant look, combine an imitation mink with a rayon bullion fringe. For a more casual look, combine an imitation sheepskin or man-made novelty fur with a cotton fringe.

Many synthetic furs can be washed and dried by machine; if you plan to use this care method, select a fringe that is also machine washable. Apply liquid fray preventer to the heading of the fringe and allow it to dry before cutting the fringe; this prevents raveling.

Because synthetic furs are bulky, it may be necessary to adjust the tension on the sewing machine. Test the straight stitch on fabric scraps, and loosen the needle thread tension as necessary for a balanced stitch. For easier construction, use a seam allowance that is the same width as the heading of the fringe. The finished throw measures about 59" (149.8 cm) square, not including the fringe.

✂ Cutting Directions

Cut a 60" (152.5 cm) square of synthetic fur with the backing side up. Cut a 59½" (151 cm) square of lining fabric.

YOU WILL NEED

1¾ yd. (1.6 m) synthetic fur, 60" (152.5 cm) wide.

1¾ yd. (1.6 m) lining fabric, 60" (152.5 cm) wide.

7 yd. (6.4 m) fringe trim.

How to Sew a Synthetic Fur Throw

1) Pin fringe to fur, with edge of heading along the edge of fabric; smooth pile in the direction of the nap, and ease the heading around the corners.

2) Fold ¾" (2 cm) back at the ends of heading; butt the folded ends. Machine-baste along the lower edge of heading.

3) Pin-mark fur and lining fabrics at center of each side. Pin lining to fur, right sides together, matching raw edges and pin marks; the nap of fur and lining should run in the same direction.

4) Stitch just inside the previous stitching, fur side up, checking for pins; leave an opening on one side for turning.

5) Trim seam allowances diagonally across corners; do not cut through trim. Shear the pile from the seam allowances at corners.

6) Turn throw right side out through opening. Gently pull fringe to shape corners. Slipstitch opening closed.

Lap Quilts ✴ ✴

This generously sized lap quilt uses a patterned striped fabric and easy strip piecing to make a quilt top that looks intricate. Six pieced strips are separated with sashing, cut from the striped fabric; and a mitered border, also cut from the striped fabric, frames the quilt.

For the sashing and border, choose a patterned striped fabric that can be cut lengthwise into strips. Most quilt shops carry suitable designs. The fabrics may include florals, paisleys, and other motifs. In order to cut the sashing and border strips from one length of fabric, you will need a striped fabric from which you can cut five sashing strips and four border strips.

The six pieced fabric strips that alternate with the sashing strips are made from six coordinating fabrics. When selecting the fabric colors, look for light, medium, and dark fabrics.

The finished size of the lap quilt varies, depending on the width of the sashing and border. The quilt shown opposite measures 56" × 68" (142 × 173 cm); the sashing has a finished width of 3½" (9 cm) and the border has a finished width of 4¼" (10.8 cm).

Use ¼" (6 mm) seam allowances in the instructions that follow. Stitch accurately, so the pieces will fit exactly. If you have a seam guide on your sewing machine, check the placement of the ¼" (6 mm) mark by stitching on a scrap of fabric. If the machine does not have a ¼" (6 mm) seam guide, mark one on the bed of the machine with tape.

✂ Cutting Directions

Cut the patterned striped fabric lengthwise to make four border strips and five sashing strips; the cut width of the strips is equal to the desired finished width plus ½" (1.3 cm) for two ¼" (6 mm) seam allowances. The cut length of the sashing strips is 60½" (153.8 cm). The border strips will be trimmed to the correct length on page 123, step 6.

Cut each of the ½-yd. (0.5 m) fabric pieces into four 3" (7.5 cm) strips, cutting the strips on the crosswise grain.

Cut the binding fabric into 2½" (6.5 cm) strips, cutting the strips on the crosswise grain.

Patterned striped fabric is cut lengthwise to make four border strips and five sashing strips. Use the design of the fabric as a guide for determining the width of the strips, and add ¼" (6 mm) seam allowance on each side of the strips.

YOU WILL NEED

2¼ yd. (2.1 m) patterned striped fabric, for sashing and border.

Six fabrics, ½ yd. (0.5 m) each, for pieced strips, in prints to coordinate with patterned striped fabric.

⅝ yd. (0.6 m) fabric, for binding.

3½ yd. (3.2 m) fabric, for backing.

Low-loft quilt batting in twin size.

Safety pins, for basting quilt layers.

1) **Stitch** together, lengthwise, one 3" (7.5 cm) strip of each fabric for the pieced strips, with right sides together and in the desired sequence. Repeat three more times, stitching in the same sequence, to make four pieced units. Press all seam allowances in the same direction.

2) **Fold** one pieced fabric unit in half crosswise. Cut the pieced unit crosswise into 5½" (14 cm) strips to make six strips; discard excess fabric. Repeat for the remaining pieced units to make twenty-four strips.

3) **Stitch** four strips together, end to end, in same sequence, to make one strip of twenty-four pieces of fabric. Repeat five times to make a total of six pieced fabric strips.

4) **Place** one sashing strip and one pieced strip right sides together; match and pin centers and ends. Pin along the length, easing in any excess fullness; stitch.

5) **Stitch** another pieced strip to the other side of the sashing. Continue stitching strips together, alternating sashing and pieced strips, until six pieced strips and five sashing strips are stitched together. Press seam allowances toward sashing.

6) Measure quilt top across middle. Cut two border strips, with length equal to this measurement plus two times finished width of border plus 1" (2.5 cm); cut width is equal to finished width of border plus ½" (1.3 cm). Repeat for side strips, measuring down the middle from top to bottom.

7) Mark center of quilt top at upper and lower edges; mark center of upper and lower border strips. From each end of border strips, mark the finished width of the border plus ½" (1.3 cm). Place upper border strip on quilt top, right sides together, matching pin marks at center.

8) Match markings at ends of strip to edges of quilt top; pin. Pin along length, easing in any fullness. Stitch, beginning and ending ¼" (6 mm) from edges of quilt top; backstitch at ends. Repeat at lower edge.

9) Repeat steps 7 and 8 for the sides of the quilt top.

10) Fold the quilt top diagonally at corner, with right sides together and matching border seamlines; pin securely. Draw a diagonal line on the border strip, extending the line formed by fold of quilt top.

(Continued on next page)

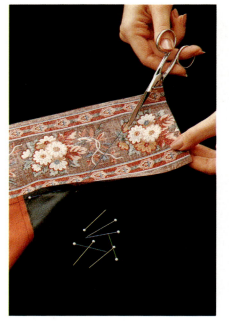

11) Stitch on the marked line; do not catch the seam allowances in stitching. Trim ends of border strips to ¼" (6 mm) from stitching.

12) Press seam allowances open at corner; press the remaining seam allowances toward the border strip. Repeat for remaining corners.

13) Cut the backing fabric 4" to 8" (10 to 20.5 cm) larger than quilt top; piece fabric as necessary and trim off selvages before stitching. Place backing wrong side up on a flat surface; tape backing taut, from center of each side, toward corners.

14) Center batting on backing. Place quilt top, right side up, on batting. Smooth, but do not stretch. Baste layers together, using safety pins, working from center out, and placing pins about every 6" (15 cm). Remove tape from backing.

15) Quilt by stitching along border strips, then along seamlines of sashing strips and pieced sections. Apply binding (opposite).

How to Apply the Binding to the Lap Quilt

1) Stitch two binding strips together, stitching seam on the bias; trim the seam allowances to ¼" (6 mm). Repeat for the remaining strips to make four binding strips. Press binding strips in half lengthwise, wrong sides together.

2) Measure quilt top across middle. Cut two binding strips equal to this measurement plus 2" (5 cm). Mark binding strips 1" (2.5 cm) from ends; divide area between pins in fourths, and pin-mark. Divide upper and lower edges of quilt in fourths; pin-mark.

3) Pin binding strip to upper edge of quilt top, matching raw edges and pin marks; binding will extend 1" (2.5 cm) beyond ends of quilt top at each end. Stitch a scant ¼" (6 mm) from raw edges.

4) Trim excess batting and backing to a scant ½" (1.3 cm) from the stitching. Wrap binding strip snugly around edge of quilt, covering the stitching line on back of quilt; pin in the ditch of the seam.

5) Stitch in the ditch on the right side of quilt top by stitching over the seamline in the well of seam; catch binding on back of quilt in the stitching.

6) Repeat steps 3 to 5 for the lower edge of quilt. Trim ends of upper and lower binding strips even with edges of quilt top.

7) Repeat steps 2 and 3 for sides. Trim the ends of the binding strips to extend ½" (1.3 cm) beyond the finished edges of the quilt. Trim the excess batting and backing to scant ½" (1.3 cm) from stitching.

8) Fold the ½" (1.3 cm) end of the binding over finished edge. Wrap binding to back of quilt and stitch as in steps 4 and 5. Slipstitch ends.

Index

Cy DeCosse Incorporated offers
a variety of how-to books. For
information write:
Cy DeCosse Subscriber Books
5900 Green Oak Drive
Minnetonka, MN 55343